LOVING
Eric

LOVING

Eric

A Story about Adoption,
Attachment, Autism & ADHD

LAURA MORRISSEY

Copyright © Laura Morrissey, 2017

The right of Laura Morrissey to be identified as the author of this work has been asserted by her in accordance with the Copyright, Designs and Patents Act 1988.

All rights reserved.
No part of this publication may be reproduced, stored in a retrieval system or transmitted in any form or by any means (electronic, mechanical, photocopying, recording or otherwise), without the prior written permission of the author.

Editorial & Design Services: The Write Factor
www.thewritefactor.co.uk

ISBN: 978-1-5455-3993-4

To My Mum

CONTENTS

Foreword		ix
Acknowledgements		xi
Author's Note		xiii
Chapter 1	My Life	1
Chapter 2	Why Do I Feel So Bad?	8
Chapter 3	The Journey Into Adoption	11
Chapter 4	The Storm	24
Chapter 5	Unstoppable Anger	28
Chapter 6	Eric and Primary School	32
Chapter 7	Eric and Secondary School	42
Chapter 8	Shame	46
Chapter 9	The Situation at Home	55
Chapter 10	The Changing Face of Adoption	67
Chapter 11	Trauma and Secondary Trauma	75
Chapter 12	Education and the Insecurely Attached, Traumatised Child	88
Chapter 13	Attachment Disorder	92
Chapter 14	Seeking Help But Gaining Labels	103
Chapter 15	Acceptance and Hope	116

Chapter 16	The Crisis	122
Chapter 17	Diary Of Events Following The Allegation	138
Chapter 18	Therapy At Last!	169
Chapter 19	New Inspiration	182
Chapter 20	The Moles in October	189
Chapter 21	Eric In The Round	207
Chapter 22	In Conclusion	210
About the Author		213
Glossary		215
References		218
Useful References & Reading		220

FOREWORD

Every word of this candid book is true. It is an honest story of adoption from the inside track. Funny, warm-hearted and ultimately full of love and hope, it also takes the reader to moments of deep, deep despair.

Laura is my sister and Eric is my nephew. As Laura was writing this book to help process her own feelings, I was privileged to read her blogs as the story unfolded. My inbox would ping and I knew I had to make a coffee and sit and read her latest accounts and offer what little hope, help, holding or insight I could as Eric's story developed like a detective novel.

For a long time I had been encouraging Laura to write about her experiences, but it was all too raw – a living, loving nightmare – which she could not share until she felt, after all of her extensive reading and research, that she had found some answers. These answers are now framed in her establishment of the Hummingbird Centre and in her discovery of Lifespan Integration Therapy (see Glossary & Links at the end of this book for more details).

Most importantly, this is a critical book for professionals, carers and families who live and work alongside adopted children, who, in addition to the trauma, separation and loss of their early years, often struggle with special educational needs. These adoptive families need new understanding to support their much-wanted child and to keep themselves and their own relationships together. Sadly, 80% of couples separate under the pressure of adoption, merely compounding loss after loss for an adopted child. Carers and professionals need to step up and confront this challenge, to courageously reflect when more of the same is not working and creatively explore alternative ways of thinking, seeing and working with families who are already on their knees.

I recommend this book to anyone who is living with this situation or working in this field in order to fill the gaps in empathy, help and practical support, because this is not just Eric's story, but it's one that is sadly repeated, again and again. This book is a call for action – for us all to do better.

Warmly,

Elaine Patterson

Executive Coach

ACKNOWLEDGEMENTS

This book would not have ever been started or completed if not for Eric! I have written it to help other parents, families, children and professionals, to show them the depth of love required to parent and fight for such a complex child.

My mum had a special relationship with Eric and would support me, shoring me up in the belief that I was a good mum, even when I felt that this could not be the case. Mum always said she could see Eric as a young man, towering over me, but walking with his arm draped over my shoulders. This image stayed in my mind's eye. Mum has travelled with me.

Derm has always been my anchor. The most non-judgemental man I have ever known and the fact that we are still together and strong as a couple is testament to our love for each other. My girls have supported me and endured many behaviours from Eric that they should not have had to, but, nevertheless, they have loved him. I admire their strength.

If not for my sister (Aunty Elaine!) this book would not have been published. Elaine has encouraged me in my writing and has been nothing, but supportive on reading my latest submissions. She has always been there for me, Derm and my three children, offering kindness, empathy and tangible support in the form of the only respite we have ever received.

My friends are really important to me. They have supported all of us throughout the last 15 years. Jeanette is my friend from Year 7 at High School and, even though we do not see each other regularly, we will always be there for each other when it counts – that is invaluable. Clare is Eric's godmother and has supported me on a pretty much a daily basis: coffee and tears in many locations, with wise words to alleviate despair. Shelf (Michele) is a constant in my life, always ready to give anything that she can; she has a lovely heart. Thanks also to Gill who is kind and generous at all times.

Sue Hawkins – Educational Psychologist and so much more – saved our family and sanity. If not for her, I would not have found Lifespan Integration Therapy or seen the changes in Eric that I have witnessed.

Andy Ruddick, Eric's lead teacher in the Hub, has also helped transform our lives. Eric needed to be understood at school and liked, both of which he is now!

AUTHOR'S NOTE

People kept asking me to write a book about adoption, attachment and Lifespan Integration Therapy (LI). I knew I had a lot to say, but I wasn't sure if I could focus long enough to pull it all together into one coherent whole. I wrote most of this book as I went along – often after key, traumatic events – because I realised that I needed to find a way of discharging the build-up of grief and anger. I could not afford for it to consume me, though at times it did.

Writing became my release, a way of processing my feelings. I have written some of these pages reflectively, with the gift of hindsight. Some chapters include practical information about the issues covered and other chapters are in their original form – that of a diary entry.

I am calling my son Eric here, as that was an affectionate name I used before meeting him when I was aware on some level that my family would only be complete when I had three children. When I talked about publishing this book about him, he asked that I use this name.

I am hoping that my journey will give comfort to some readers and a recognition that they are not alone. I hope that if any professionals read it, they will reflect on their practice and open their hearts and minds so that they become more curious, reflective practitioners.

Finally, I wanted to share some of my hard-won answers and encourage others to fight for themselves and their children – because they all deserve support in the tumultuous seas of their life and guidance to find their own safe harbours.

1

MY LIFE

I have decided to start this book by giving a brief insight into our family life – in this case a particular incident during a half-term holiday. My family and my sister, Elaine, and her daughter, my niece, Naomi, had decided to head off to the Lake District for May half-term in 2014. We were staying at Lymefitt Park in two separate lodges, the park itself being situated in a beautiful, relaxing setting, yet with loads of activities to do if we felt like it. We had agreed that I would drive up a few hours before my husband, Dermot, and our son, Eric, and our eldest daughter, Jess, would follow on later.

I drove up with my middle daughter, Zoe, a girl who rarely speaks freely, which I feel is down to a combination of being the middle child, her need to find her own path and also being subjected to Eric and his incessant talking! On this particular day, however, Zoe and I talked all the way there and I really enjoyed this special time together. She is interesting and deep, once you can get her talking.

When we arrived, Zoe helped put all our belongings away in the lodge's various wardrobes and cupboards. I thought she was joking when she said, "You do realise that Eric has only brought pants and pyjamas?" I had placed all of his clothes ready on his bed and we had agreed that he would put them in the case I had left out for him. It transpired that she was not joking about his clothing situation and when asked about this later, Eric said, "I couldn't fit it all in the bag, so I left it". Logical, perhaps – but helpful? Sadly not! We always encouraged Eric to take responsibility for himself, in this case packing his own bags, but here we learned yet another lesson: that Eric had no comprehension that he could've chosen a bigger bag for his belongings or asked for help. I knew it would mean a trip to Bowness on Windermere in the morning to buy Eric enough clothes for the holiday. It was an expensive mistake, but not catastrophic.

Dermot, Eric and Jess all arrived later that evening. Eric was stressed and could not stop talking and asking question after question. It didn't matter what he was saying, he just needed to speak. I recognised that this was just his stress being spewed out and I reflected that to him, which seemed to help somewhat and he started to settle into his new environment. It reminded me that every change was a potential trauma to my nearly 12-year old boy. For him, excitement is too close to the feeling of fear.

The holiday went well and Eric only got grumpy a few times, mostly because he was fairly free to roam the campsite at will, as it was safe and secure. He had one bout of bad temper when he wanted to stay at my sister's lodge and sleep on the small settee. We said no – that we thought he'd be more comfortable in his own bed – and he was unhappy about that, but he didn't make too much fuss, considering Eric detests being told that he can't always do things he wants to do.

Eric and I were due to leave on the Saturday, Dermot and the girls having left on the Friday due to various social commitments. I stayed on with my sister, niece and Eric for one more day. Eric cried as his father and sisters left and I realised that this was a manifestation of change kicking in and impacting on his feelings of security. His tears were exacerbated by the fact that Dermot would not allow him to use any more hair gel as he had too much in already! I talked with Eric about the hair gel and we agreed that he could use it in smaller amounts – and I told him that I would speak to Dad about this and make sure this was okay with him too. I was mostly trying to calm Eric down with this compromise, recognising that he was feeling anxious and, therefore, angry, as, for him, the two emotions live side by side and feed each other. The hair gel was not the real issue.

My sister and I and our two charges left the lodge for our final day of the holiday. We ate breakfast out, walked along Rydal Water for two hours, had tea and cake and then returned to the lodge. We'd had a nice day. I had a quick power nap and Eric played outside with his cousin and talked to his aunty. He came to tell me that tea was ready at 7pm and then the requests to stay the night with my sister in her lodge began again.

I said no, due to the fact we were leaving the next day and there was no proper bed for him – he couldn't share with his 13-year old female cousin. All through tea, Eric went on and on about staying with his aunty in her lodge, mumbling under his breath and poking at me incessantly. He would not stop. We cleared up after the meal, whilst he sat and moaned. We watched some TV and still he moaned. Eventually, by 9pm, I'd had enough. I had tried reasoning with him, play-fighting with him, cajoling him … all these approaches were massively unsuccessful.

We left to go back to our lodge, with me holding onto his arm. I didn't put it past him to run off and cause a scene. On the way back, he said I was fat and needed to lose weight. He said he wished he lived with his birth mum, not me. She would let him smoke and drink and take drugs – he could do whatever he liked with his birth mum. He said he no longer wanted to live with us. Back at the lodge, he ranted on. He slammed doors and continued to abuse me. He refused to calm down, get washed or clean his teeth, the tirade continuing until gone 10.45pm. Eventually, he retired to bed, but I sat up until midnight, feeling upset, deskilled and depressed.

Saturday morning arrived and I was met with more anger and aggression: Eric refusing to get up, to get dressed, to pack or to wash. In the end, I packed everything up and helped my sister put her bike and bike rack on her car, but I locked him in the lodge whilst doing this, for fear of him absconding, a feeling of impotence lying heavily in my chest, choking me. How could a 12-year old boy make me feel so powerless?

When I returned to the lodge ten minutes later, Eric was dressed and partially packed, but hadn't washed or cleaned his teeth. Still, it was a step in the right direction. His mood remained aggressive: he shouted at me as we left the lodge and then, to my amazement, he waved at the neighbours very politely as he skipped to the car! It confirmed my suspicion that he was intent on punishing me, but was also another example of him being able to switch from one mood to another at will. He hated strangers to see the argumentative Eric. We drove into Windermere for breakfast, with Eric insisting it was all my fault for not letting him stay at his aunt's lodge – in effect, because I said "No" to him. I explained that sometimes in life you can't always get what you want and that's just the way it is and that he needed to find a way of coping with that. I talked about how our thoughts affect how we feel and then how we behave and that our behaviour has consequences and can hurt others – but it had little impact on Eric as he was too deeply entrenched in his anxiety/anger cycle, a place where reason does not exist. We ate breakfast with my sister and drove home in silence.

At home, Eric objected to helping out with any of the chores. He threw his stuff in his room, but that was it. He refused to help empty the dishwasher or tidy up the house with me, but I was no longer sure how to discipline him for refusing to do as he was asked. He'd already incrementally been banned from using the computer, from visiting his surrogate grandmother and from going to the BMX track on his own – all because of his bad behaviour. Each escalation of unacceptable behaviour created yet another consequence for him, one step at a time – but it didn't seem to make any difference. I had arranged for him to meet with a friend on the coming Monday after school at the BMX track, but this now hung very much in the balance. In the face of his challenging behaviour, Eric is warned and given many alternatives and other ways out, so that he does not feel penned in, but when he is angry, he is unable to hear these options and descends deeper into his emotional turmoil. Consequences do not matter to him at this time. I always follow the sanctions through, but sometimes I feel that I am the one being punished instead of him because the impact of him not being allowed to do something sentences me to more one-to-one time with an aggressive young man. Despite the fact that consequences are ineffective for Eric, I have always believed that he has to learn that actions result in certain outcomes because in the adult world, leeway would not be given. I want him to learn that his behaviour is unacceptable and also point out that, when he is calm, I can tell him exactly why he cannot do something and he accepts it – and if I ever gave in to him, he would (quite rightly) point out that he had got away with something! So the rules are there, visible, consistent and firm. Boundaries are there for him to kick against, but ultimately these are the things that make the attachment-disordered child feel safe.

Instead of coming home from our holiday refreshed and relaxed, I just felt angry and exhausted. Once again, Eric had reduced a happy family time to one of stress and disappointment. It all ends up being about him and his mood.

2

WHY DO I FEEL SO BAD?

I have been reflecting on why I feel so tired today – like the stuffing has been knocked out of me again. At times like this, it feels as if the future is bleak, everything is a struggle and I am lonely. I am back in that place of complete exhaustion, as if every day is a massive confrontation, – and, thinking about it, that's true: each day is a battle.

I always love to research and learn more. Whilst researching attachment issues I read about secondary trauma and realised that this described exactly how I was feeling – the trauma of living with Eric and his anger for the last 9.5 years. It has taken its toll. Every incident where I feel that I cannot control his rage and have to absorb it takes me back to all the years of fighting with him and for him. I am experiencing re-traumatisation. The effects are wearing, tiring. I question my ability and feel that I fail daily.

Secondary trauma is like an overfull glass, filled to the rim with toxicity. One more incident just adds to this toxicity, making the liquid that is barely contained in the vessel overflow. Emotion, in the form of tears, overflows from my eyes in much the same way, a leaking that, up until this time with Eric, I had never experienced. I wasn't a 'crier' – in fact, crying in my family was seen as a weakness. If ever I said that I had an issue at school or with a friend, my mum would say, "You didn't cry in front of them did you?" The answer was always no.

I also knew the root of these tears. The fact is that, unfortunately, holidays for Eric cause stress. Change causes stress. Life causes stress and Eric deals with stress via wild explosions of aggression and abuse aimed at those around him – although not usually strangers: he keeps his aggression for his family or school peers (he does not have friends of his own and the only people he plays with are the sons of my friends). Professionals always state, somewhat simplistically in my view, the importance of remaining calm and focusing on the trauma the child suffered, not the behaviour. But the trauma being wrought on me is ignored, as, after all, he is the child and I am the adult – and adults are expected to cope. This is easier said than done though! I know I must now regroup again so that I can care for him and our two other vulnerable children. There is no rest for me – I am here with Eric on my own until my husband returns from work. Dermot works shifts, so out of five weekends, he would normally only have two off. Unfortunately, shifts are draining and, in addition to this, Dermot suffers from appalling migraines that are debilitating, often impacting him so much on the weekends that he's at home that he would need to rest most of the time. How do I look after myself at these times?

This is why adopters of children with trauma in their DNA need specialist support. They need a network to help them; they need time to heal and revitalise, so they can head into battle again, and again – because the battles are never-ending. They exist both at home with the child and externally with the educators, social workers and any other "professionals" involved (and I use that term loosely) in their care.

I love my son with all my heart and I will always persevere, one way or another to help and support him, but I am more mindful of my limits now. I will rest when Dermot returns from work and I do not see this as weak, but, rather, as a necessity in order that I can continue to parent Eric.

3

THE JOURNEY INTO ADOPTION

I never really knew whether I wanted children or not until I got into my late twenties. Before that, when thinking of having children, I was more career-orientated. However, I did not see having children and having a career as being mutually exclusive. I joined the police force after university. I was quickly promoted to sergeant and met my husband to be, Dermot, at work at the age of 22. I was 27 when we got married. I left the police after seven years, the contributing factors being boredom, restlessness and a lack of fulfilment – and the vague thought that if we did have children, shift work would not suit me. I didn't want ours to be the kind of family where the parents had to juggle childcare between one shift and another.

Police work is hard and thankless. I was exposed to the harsh underbelly of life in council estates at the tender age of 21. I had never before experienced violence or drug and domestic abuse. Being on duty, walking through Salford on my own at night was an eye-opener. In 1986, when I joined GMP, probationers, both male and female, were expected to walk the precinct area on their own for the whole of an eight-hour shift. It taught me that I had to be able to communicate with all walks of life; it taught me how to make small talk, how to engage people – and these skills have paid off throughout my life. Most importantly, it taught me to respect other people, regardless of their circumstances.

My heart softened upon being exposed to the victims of crime, most notably, the elderly who lived alone in their tower block flats. I wanted to help them more than my role allowed. Perhaps my desire to be instrumental in changing their lives for the better was naïve? Perhaps if I knew then what I know now, I would have stayed in the police? I was a good police officer, but, nonetheless, I was restless and unfulfilled. Also the shiftwork and stress levels caused severe irritable bowel syndrome, so much so that I would often throw up on night shift and then resume patrol. Gynaecologically, all was not well either, adding further complications to an already complex job.

Some people were very surprised by my decision to leave the police because I was considered to be on the "promotion path" and I think they thought I was throwing my life away. I started working for a charity, Alternative Futures, based in Liverpool and Cheshire, but this was disillusioning in the extreme: standards were difficult to maintain, change was strongly resisted and promotion, although promised, went to other colleagues. During this time, Dermot and I had decided to try and start a family, but I was already experiencing difficulties in conceiving and when I decided to leave that organisation, the Chief Executive asked me if I was only seeking promotion because I was unable to have children. That hurt. He also said that I would soon return, asking for my job back. I did not.

I then worked as an operations manager for Mencap and covered for my boss, who suffered from a year-long bout of ill health. The charity went through a reorganisation process every three years, regardless of whether it needed to or not, and a new principal manager, who became my boss, was appointed. This manager had very little experience and also suffered from multiple sclerosis. It seemed that she took an instant dislike to me, even though she did not know me, and, for this reason, I did not respect her, but, of course, I was willing to give our working relationship my best shot. I covered for her when she went off sick shortly after being appointed, but all the thanks I got was her questioning my timekeeping.

Whilst at Mencap, I was diagnosed as having severe endometriosis, thus conception was a remote possibility. My womb, that should apparently 'float' was, in fact, rock solid. I often felt very ill and had suffered for years because every time I had a period I was in severe, crippling pain. My insides felt as if they were being scaled out by sharp nails and I had to be very careful not to over-medicate with painkillers. I felt exhausted for whole weeks at a time. In the end, I decided that life was too short to continue like this, limping from month to month, with little or no chance of conceiving.

After much thought and discussion with Dermot, I decided to request a hysterectomy as all other treatments on offer were ineffective or actually made things worse. I wanted to feel well. Also, as I had grown up around adoption – our family friends had adopted three children – the prospect of adopting, rather than conceiving children, seemed normal to me. My husband took longer to come around to the idea, but, in the end, we were in complete agreement.

As I went in for my hysterectomy, we applied to adopt and proceeding with the adoption process helped me to come to terms with the trauma of this life-changing operation: I decided to look ahead, which gave me a degree of control, seeing the prospect of having a family and of having a purpose.

In 1999, we attended a series of adoption classes run by the Manchester Adoption Society (MAS), where we met with Lynne, our social worker, and started the assessment side that goes with adoption. During the approval process, you have to state whether you could adopt one or more children and we said that we ideally wanted have a sibling group of two children. At this point, we had no idea about the gender or ages of our prospective children. The process took a year and was really very invasive – it is not for the faint-hearted – and our families and friends were examined in detail. Initially, we opted for the Goodman scheme. This meant that we would initially foster and meet up with the birth parents three times a week, whist they underwent help to see if they could properly parent their children.

Birth families are given every conceivable help and, in effect, we were to be babysitters whilst the courts decided the children's fate. This meant that if the children were reunited with their parents, we, the foster family, would lose them for good. But it was a job we were willing to do, as we believed, and still do, that the child benefits. How we would have coped if the children were returned, happily we never had to find out.

However, Lynne, changed teams and left Goodman to become part of the main adoption team. As we had built up a relationship with her and trusted her, we opted to transfer with her. After approval, we waited a year to hear about a suitable placement. Because we wanted siblings, it took longer to find a suitable match. The year was hard to endure and, with no movement forward, it felt like being suspended in time. Planning was complex – could we book a holiday, for example, or would we get the call? It was as if we were permanently on stand by, ready to become parents. At the time, this felt like the worst period in the adoption process, the limbo between approval and placement. We were waiting for our family, but had no timescale or knowledge of the children's age or gender. It was extremely difficult, being in that frame of mind, as we could not visualise who our children would be.

In the interim, I took on more responsibility at Mencap. During the time that my boss was on sick leave for a year, I filled in for her unofficially. I compiled reports and attended national meetings to keep the Northwest area ticking along. I didn't receive extra pay or even any appreciation, but it kept me busy. In my third year there, during the obligatory Mencap reorganisation, all of the key jobs were sent to an externally run (and, it has to be said, expensive) Assessment Centre.

I applied for a more senior role and went to Birmingham to have feedback on my application at the Assessment Centre. The day before, I'd had an impacted molar removed and I was still in considerable pain, but I went anyway. It turned out that I was not considered for the role I'd applied for and the feedback from the Centre was massively unhelpful. All I was told was that I had answered the questions well, but not well enough. There was a lack of specificity, meaning that I was not clear as to where I had gone wrong and how I could improve in future – although I did wonder if my application failed due to my impending adoption leave. Due to my apparent failure, I was put on a management course for a few days.

The course was okay, involving team games and raft-building. However, I was no clearer by the end of the course as to why I did not get promoted than when I started! As I was about to get in my car at the end of the course, I had a phone call from Dermot to say that Lynne had been in contact about two sisters who were two-and-a-half and one-and-a-half years old whom she felt would be a great match for us and vice versa. At last – the adoption was finally going ahead! Perhaps things happen for a reason? I could hardly drive home safely enough or fast enough. It was an amazing feeling! All my other feelings of being not quite good enough faded into the background as my attention became focused on making a safe, secure family for our two little girls. I always wanted girls, but had never admitted this during the adoption assessments. I am not really sure why.

My sister, Elaine, came out with us for lunch in Wilmslow that Saturday. Dermot and I held onto our secret, so that we could share it with Elaine and my mum. However, Elaine saw our adoption worker, Lynne, on the high street and she was about to run after her to find out what was going on with our placement. We stopped her and told her that we had some news and were about to have two little girls placed with us. We rang Mum, who got straight in her car and drove over to celebrate with us.

After another interminable wait, during which the girls' social worker visited us and kept rather unhelpfully telling me that Zoe was now walking and other developmental milestones that we were missing due to the slow turning of the bureaucratic wheels. The Adoption Panel eventually approved the match and we went to meet our daughters in Leyland that very day. Lynne asked us what we thought after our introduction. I just felt love and wanted to take them home that day! The introductions lasted over two weeks, during which we had to travel to see them daily, 45 minutes each way. On getting home, we had to buy and erect the nursery furniture and, as ever, the DIY didn't go smoothly! We couldn't buy it ahead of time as we didn't know the gender or age of our children until the match was made and any decision is not final until after the Adoption Panel agrees. Everything is so last-minute in adoption and, for someone like myself, who likes a plan, it felt particularly challenging.

Eventually, the girls came home with us for good in June 2001. It was surreal and wonderful at the same time. I gave up work for the requisite year, the time MAS recommends in order to bond securely with the children. I went from a full-time manager to a housewife overnight and I had none of the usual preparations: I was not pregnant, so had no need to slow down and, unlike most other women, I had no baby shower, no good luck cards ... it was a strange time. There is no formula or rite of passage for adopters: suddenly, you are a family. Interestingly, I discovered pretty quickly that people lose interest in you when they discover that you are a non-working mum – perhaps because I no longer had an external role that defined me.

Life was suddenly full on. My daughters were high energy – on the go from 5am until bedtime – it seemed they had no need for sleep during the day. The girls were full of life and took everything on at full tilt. They settled in well at home and seemed to adjust quickly to their new life. The social workers recommended that Jess and Zoe had contact visits with their two older siblings who were in foster care at the time. We were happy to do this twice a year and we met up in the Lake District and Leeds, finding different venues to suit the four children who loved to meet up!

Jess was quiet and seemed quite serious, but Zoe seemed to bring her out of herself. Zoe was always full of mischief. I had to have two travel cots, one upstairs and one downstairs, so I could keep them in one place when need be. Very quickly, the travel cot became Jessica's jigsaw play area, stopping Zoe from wrecking it!

I gradually found activities for the girls and realised that this was the best way for me to connect with other mums who had children of a similar age, as all of my previous friends lived further away or worked full-time. I realised that all of us were happiest when busy, outside and having treats in the local cafés! This also helped Dermot to sleep during the day because when they were bored they would run around in circles in the lounge, becoming noisier and noisier.

The adjustment from full-time work to full-time motherhood had been an interesting journey. I loved the girls wholeheartedly and realised that I was happy being at home with them. I did intend to go back to Mencap, but, after a year off, things had changed at work and Zoe did not cope with nursery when we introduced her to it. I decided, after the year-long adoption leave, to resign and be at home with them until they were older. I had found other mums with children of similar ages to connect with and activities and groups that the girls enjoyed. As they grew older, they were sporty and threw themselves into everything – Jess first, then Zoe, but only after standing back and assessing everything!

In 2003, we decided we would adopt a boy. We wanted a larger family and felt we had coped remarkably well parenting our two girls – and we also felt that there was enough love to go around. In retrospect, it's fair to say we had no idea of the journey we were embarking upon. Again, the bureaucracy kicked into action: we were assessed as a family and eventually approved – and, after another year of waiting, we met Eric in October 2004. He was two years and four months old. He looked like me, or so everyone commented at the initial meeting.

Eric had been removed from his birth mother at hospital, meaning that he never actually lived with her. We were informed that her six other children had already been adopted and the identity of Eric's birth father was unclear. His birth mum (let's call her Amy) had learning disabilities and had been 'groomed' by an older man. Her first four children had been horribly neglected – left without food, locked in a cupboard, living in a house where urine ran through the ceiling above – and they had been rescued eventually, but I am sure the damage to them is ongoing. Amy was sent to prison for her part in the neglect – a highly unusual event in the child protection world – but, on leaving prison, she went on to have three more children.

Eric was placed with a foster family who had two older children after leaving hospital. After that, he was transported via taxi, on his own, to a Social Services venue to have contact with Amy three times a week. The thought of him going off in the taxi on his own as a baby brought tears to my eyes. These visits went well because they were supervised – so well, in fact, that the court psychologist deemed Amy fit enough to parent Eric. His contact with her increased to daily over the intervening weeks and they was set to reunite mother and son. However, Amy was then found by the police drunk and lying in the gutter whilst being responsible for her two nephews and this put an end to this plan. Contact between them stopped abruptly. He suffered a massive loss that was never explained to him and she just disappeared from his life. He would have and is still unable to communicate about this loss on a cognitive level, but his body feels a "somatic" or body-held loss. Each trauma we experience is held within the body and remembered until it is processed into the narrative parts of our brains. The loss of a birth mother is a trauma in itself.

We were informed that another couple had been matched up with Eric before us, but that had fallen through when they discovered that Friedreich's Ataxia ran in the family. Amy's sister and her sons had it. Friedreich's Ataxia is a life-limiting wasting disease that kills those affected by it by the time they reach 18 years of age. We were sent to see a geneticist to discuss the risks. Apparently, both parents have to be carriers in order for it to be passed on to their children – however, in our case, we did not know who Eric's dad was and the man believed to be his dad would not submit to the screening test for paternity or any genetic enquiry about the potentially inheritable disease.

Even in the face of this information, we proceeded with the adoption. The chances were that he would not be affected, but really our decision was based on nothing more than hope. I am amazed on looking back, that we still continued – resolutely hoping for the best – intent on adding to our family. Were we blindly optimistic or just plain stupid?

Before meeting Eric, we had a long meeting with the foster family and Social Services and no concerns about his behaviour were mentioned at all. After the meeting we returned home and then arranged to rent a holiday cottage near to the foster family for the requisite two-week introductory period. The cottage turned out to be rather grim, with a mountain of steps down to it that were not easy for a two-year old to negotiate. The girls came too as it was the October half-term. We went through the introductions and felt that things were a bit strange – for example, when we arrived to collect Eric for days out, he was already suited and booted prior to our arrival at the foster home and the foster carer did not invite us in or ease the transition. Eric was handed over on the doorstep and, although he seemed content to leave, we noticed that there was no real connection with the foster mum.

We also noticed that Eric's speech was severely limited to, "Ducks, whack, whack". He did not know how to play on a slide – in fact, it looked as if he had never been to a park to play at all. During the course of the two weeks, Eric's care was handed over to us, so, for example, we went to his foster home to help with the bath/bedtime routine, but, actually, the foster mother just sat on the settee and got her 14-year old daughter to help us bathe him. He had a tantrum during one bath-time, and I was not allowed near him, but this was the only tantrum we saw – otherwise, he was almost mute. He smiled, stuck his hand up in the air to be held and stayed glued to an adult's side.

Eric was brought to our home at the end of the two weeks and the foster family left. Eric did not seem concerned at all. He fell asleep on my chest that afternoon and it felt peaceful and right. Little did I realise that this was the calm before the storm!

4

THE STORM

All was well for the first few weeks: Eric sat on my lap, smiled and was angelic, but, on reflection, he was probably traumatised and "frozen". Then the tantrums began and did not stop. The first one I will always remember as if it happened yesterday. The children and I, plus my mum had all gone to Trinity Church for the Christingle service. The candles were lit and hope filled the air for the Christmas to come. Then Eric started shouting. I removed him from the church into the kitchen area in an attempt to calm him down, but he shouted and screamed, and became red-faced and no words could soothe him – he just became more and more angry. We had to leave quickly, feeling at a loss as to what to do. Eric's tantrum had come from nowhere, but, on leaving the church, things settled down again. The second occasion was at the primary school's Christmas Fair. We were queuing to see Santa when Eric started screaming and crying again, just like in the church and as with that episode, nothing would calm him this time either. We had to accept that we would not get to see Santa!

The next memorable time was at the Trafford Centre with my friend, Clare. We had planned to take him to the play area, but, once again, a tantrum erupted out of nowhere. He kept trying to escape from us, becoming angrier at every passing minute. Promises of some time in the play area when he'd calmed down had no effect on him. He would temporarily stop this behaviour upon seeing something that interested him – it was as if someone had hit a "pause" button – but, as soon as the object of interest passed, his rage descended again. We had to admit defeat and went home.

Clare left me at home and came back several hours later, so we could collect our children from school together. She told me later that, as she walked up the drive, she could hear Eric screaming inside the house. She could hardly believe it when I told her that he had carried on like this all day and that nothing – *nothing* – appeased him. Eventually, I'd put him in his cot, and left him to it, but the screaming continued. I was at a loss, never experiencing the length or depth of such a tantrum before. Eric seemed to hardly suffer any consequences from such an extended bout of emotional expression, almost as if he was not fully engaged in the process somehow – but I was utterly exhausted by it.

Later, I tried to explain to Dermot the intensity of Eric's tantrum, but I couldn't quite describe it vividly enough. The maelstrom of emotions and anger that Eric was expressing, and the chaos it created in me, was hard to convey. What made matters worse was that, when I explained what happened to the social worker, Lynne, I felt that I was not being heard properly.

In the end, I rang his foster mum to talk about it. She said that she was not surprised to hear about his tantrums and that she thought that Eric needed psychiatric help. She said she had asked for support from Social Services and also that she had asked for him to be removed and placed elsewhere as she felt they were not coping with him. However, Social Services asked her to continue fostering Eric as a placement was on the horizon, but it resulted in Eric being with them for over two years. His tantrums meant that she no longer took him out in public as she couldn't cope with his 'meltdowns' on the bus, in shops, in playgroup, or pretty much anywhere else. And so Eric's life diminished, as she stopped taking him out, and he did not learn how to play. I was incredulous when she told me that, if he screamed, he was shut in the utility room with the dog and frequently put to bed at midday and left there until the older children returned from school at 4.30 pm. His stimulation was *Bob the Builder* on TV and his life was one of neglect.

It was all becoming clear to me now: she hadn't been truthful about the tantrums in case it put us off adopting Eric. It felt as if I had been punched in the stomach – then a feeling of utter panic overwhelmed me as I realised that this behaviour was Eric's 'normal'. To me, his anger was like unstoppable lava being spewed from the bundle of stress that was his body. The lava would vent for hours on end with no remission – unless a stranger walked in. Then the flow would be suspended, only to resume upon their departure.

I did write a letter of complaint about the foster carer's neglect and abuse of Eric and was contacted by Social Services who requested a meeting – but I refused. I was exhausted and I had put everything down in my letter of complaint: there was no more to say. I just said that I was not seeking financial compensation and that I just wanted them to tighten their controls in order to keep children safe from similar abuse, but they never contacted me again. I don't know if any action was taken to safeguard the children in the foster parents' care, but I think, at the very least, there's a need for training and guidance for foster carers faced with this kind of situation.

5

UNSTOPPABLE ANGER

Eric's anger presented as sustained aggression: screaming, banging doors and throwing anything at me in his efforts to "up the ante", using every opportunity to seek a reaction. I felt powerless. Normal strategies were useless in the face of his anger. This small person would not be corralled. The "naughty step" was useless. Time outs just inflamed the fires of his anger. Doors could not contain him. Attending toddler groups was humiliating. He would exert his will at the drop of a hat, going rigid in his rage, so that his pushchair became useless as I could not mould his little body into it, and getting him in or out of the car was a nightmare because the straps of his car seat were barely able to stop his escape.

I felt alone and hopeless. I cried in every car park we used. I felt that no one understood the level of abuse – for that was what it was – that I was subjected to day after day. I even videoed Eric in full "rage mode" to try and evidence his behaviour. We were referred to the Child and Adolescent Mental Health Services (CAMHS) in Derbyshire, but all the "help" I received was a photocopy of a report stating that, in the case of attachment disorders, the young person inevitably ended up in "borstal". No strategies were offered that would help both myself and Eric to cope. I felt that there must be a better way, a way of avoiding this black hole that my son kept falling into. No child deserved this fate.

I spoke to Lynne again as I was incensed by the lack of support I was getting. I refused to accept this situation. Lynne gave me some guidance and did some play therapy with Eric, who soon got the hang of things and used the figurines to identify us, his new family, and his foster family. The foster family were then quickly dispatched behind the floor length curtains, then later, were tellingly dropped into the bin. Lynne also came up with a hedgehog soft toy that depicted Eric in his calm and angry phases. I was pleased to see that he understood the analogy, but, unfortunately, he was unable to stop himself.

After a year, we went to court and formally adopted Eric, but I realise now that this was far too quick for our family because, basically, once the Adoption Order occurs, Social Services skip off into the ether and we were left with no resources and nobody to turn to – because, as far as they are concerned, it was a "job done". We still had Lynne, our MAS social worker, to lean on, but all too soon, MAS lost funding and shut down. The reason for going ahead after a year, even though things were extremely difficult, was mainly to do with Eric's social worker from Derbyshire. Adopted children have their own worker responsible for their placement and they have to make statutory visits to ensure the welfare of the child. She had taken over his case just prior to his placement with us. She was a newly qualified and inexperienced social worker and, unfortunately, Eric associated her with loss. Every time she visited us – following the basic statutory requirements – the result was at least two weeks of even worse behaviour from Eric. Each time she came, she insisted on discussing his behaviour in front of him – in effect, shaming him. I explained this to her, but she refused to believe me. Eric clearly didn't like her and this was an emotion I came to mirror because she would not listen to me or be flexible in her approach to our needs.

I explained the impact of her visits to her, joining up the dots for her, so to speak, but she just reported to her managers that I was "stressed", that I was not coping, that I was wrong … I think it's fair to say that we adopted Eric to get her out of our lives, but, again, in retrospect – isn't hindsight a wonderful thing! – I think that adopting after one year was a mistake: not the adoption itself, but the chronology. We knew were always going to be there for Eric as he was our son and we loved him above all else, but we needed more support due to his complexity. We hoped that, without the additional stress of the social worker visiting, we could find a way forward more easily. Derbyshire Social Services were too remote geographically to provide practical help and, at the time, we believed that MAS and Lynne in particular would always be there for us. I think that if MAS had survived, then our story would not have been as difficult.

6

ERIC AND PRIMARY SCHOOL

Eric starting primary school meant a whole new era of awfulness. His attachment issues meant that he loved, hated and feared me, and, therefore, my presence presented untold stress, but my leaving was like the end of the world for him. Whenever I left our house, there was an outbreak of screaming, rage, loss, banging on doors and windows without any fear of the damage that broken glass can wreak. Each departure left me with the imprint of a red, raging face pressed against the window-pane – a little boy beside himself with loss and grief. Once I had actually gone, he returned to calm mode, but obviously I did not see this! When I returned home, I was always met with the same rage: *How dare you leave me? You will pay dearly now.*

Any respite I felt in leaving him was destroyed as I set foot back over the threshold. I was left feeling that separation from Eric was not worth the toll it took on my return. Not that leaving him with others was easy either. As I've mentioned previously, we had no real support network surrounding us: Mum was too elderly to look after three young children on her own and my sister lives in London. In fact, on the one occasion that Dermot and I did go to the cinema, on our return, we found my mum was very upset. It transpired that Eric had not been calm and the girls had decided that the best thing to do was to lock Mum and Eric in his bedroom, leaving the phone outside of the room. They eventually liberated Mum, but she was none too happy with the experience and I felt too guilty to ask her to babysit again! The girls were in trouble with us, of course, and they knew they had been wrong in their decision to lock the door, but it meant we couldn't trust them not to repeat their misdemeanour.

School should have given me some respite – a whole day to regain my composure – but the opposite was true. Eric coped with school until Year 2, although things at home remained volatile. His Year 1 teacher, Mr. Jones, (who, unfortunately, the Head disliked intensely), was great with Eric – he just seemed to cope with him, understand him and, most importantly, like him! Eric also had a friend in Year 1 who had speech delay and Eric, who loved to talk, helped him. They were good for each other and this helped Eric to cope.

Year 2 saw him disintegrate in the face of a newly qualified teacher. She could not cope well with the class, I believe, and she cried in front of them. This seeming inability to cope made Eric feel unsafe and, therefore, he became more challenging. She always came to me in the schoolyard to recount Eric's behaviour in front of him, a pattern I saw repeating itself from his social worker to teacher. I asked her not do this, but, like the social worker from Derbyshire before her, she ignored my requests. This public shaming of Eric was very damaging. To shame someone is to make them feel deeply wounded, different, isolated and, therefore, vulnerable. Shame is a primeval response, tribal in essence, because to be excluded from the tribe meant that you were the weak link, the easy target. In the playground, this became very much the case for Eric and for myself. We became the pariahs of the playground: Eric was the "naughty boy" and I was the "bad mother" who failed to control him.

Eventually, after I made numerous representations to the head teacher, asking for more support for Eric – as I could see his behaviour spiralling out of control at school and also at home – Eric was moved into a class run by Ms. King, the Special Educational Needs Coordinator (SENCO). She understood Eric and managed to work with him.

Eric, by now, hated school and it felt like the school hated us. I managed to get an Educational Psychologist (EP) to come in, through MAS, at no cost to the school, but they were rude to her in the extreme, dismissing what she said out of hand. Judi, the EP, felt sorry for me after these meetings and really tried to help. My belief is that they felt threatened by an outside agency coming in and they refused to accept her help, leaving everyone floundering. The school were out of their depth, but unwilling to seek advice from experienced professionals, which confounded me. I found her to be excellent, but the school treated her with contempt. Eventually, this lifeline was strangled and the support stopped.

By Year 3, there was a suggestion that Eric should receive a Statement of Special Educational Needs from the Stockport Educational Psychologist, Ms. Geery. This was broached without warning in a meeting. I was really upset as this seemed to be taking us down a different route altogether. At first, I thought the Statement was a bad idea, that it labeled Eric as disabled, but I talked it over with Derm who was very pragmatic and said that if Eric needed help, we must accept it. I came to terms with this new reality, but, in the next meeting, the same EP, Ms. Geery, said that Eric did not, in fact, meet the criteria for a Statement and that avenue would not be pursued. It was bizarre: the Statement was suggested by the professionals, not us, but to then have this overturned and a rapid U-turn made between meetings was confusing, to say the least.

The only good thing for Eric was that, in Year 3, he had one-to-one support in class and at break time. This helped him to fit in and he began to develop friendships for the first time since Year 1 – and, educationally, he began to make real progress. The teachers in Years 3 and 4 'got' him. They 'team taught', so the two classrooms were open plan and there was continuity for Eric. The boundaries were also very clear.

Sadly, after Year 4, things changed: the model of 'team teaching' was mirrored, but for Years 5 and 6, the building and classroom layout was different which was a significant factor for Eric. The teachers also changed and, as had been our experience throughout, communication between teachers was not good, so that the things that had worked for Eric were not passed on to his new teachers. It was like going back to square one.

I kept saying to the lead teacher of Year 5 & 6 that his behaviour was getting worse and he needed more support, but she insisted that it was okay and that if she had him for a week, then she would single-handedly sort him out! I tried not to take offence at that comment, although it did feel like she was reproaching me for my parenting abilities. In addition to this, she would march up to both of us in the playground and regale me, in front of Eric, about all his misdemeanours. I repeatedly asked her not to, explaining the impact this had on his anxiety, self-esteem and anger levels, but she continued regardless. Every time this public telling off happened by social workers or teachers, Eric was shamed and, as a consequence, became more angry with me and the world. He hated to get things wrong, but seemed unable to adjust his behaviour. It seemed like I was forever in and out of school and that Eric was forever in trouble – and I was becoming increasingly concerned about how Eric would fare in secondary school.

To make matters worse, my mum was admitted to Wythenshawe hospital in the September of 2011. Mum

ERIC AND PRIMARY SCHOOL

had insisted on living in her own home, but was beginning to find it difficult. Then, one day, inexplicably, she began to lose her balance. Eventually, she asked me if I could come over and take her to see her doctor. Mum lived in a village called Tattenhall, eight miles south of Chester. When we were called through to see the GP, I was shocked to see that she was unable to walk down the corridor without falling into doors, bouncing from side to side like a pinball. After the appointment, we went to her house and I packed a bag for her so that she could come and stay at my house in Manchester in order that she could recuperate. Mum wasn't up to packing for herself and she just said, "Take me home with you, Laura". It was an admission as to how bad she felt. Mum never asked for help.

My last memory of Mum in her own house was a few weekends prior to this when Eric and I had gone over to see her. Her kitchen overlooked a small partially sheltered patio where Mum loved to sit, drink her coffee and read her paper. She was outside the window, having a coffee and Eric was sitting on her lap, talking and patting the back of her head as he did so. It is an image that will always stay with me, a picture of love.

Mum was in hospital for nine weeks, coming home briefly and then being rushed back in by ambulance. She lost the ability to breathe independently and had to wear a 'C Pac' mask at night that assisted her breathing by forcing air into her lungs. It terrified her. My brother-in-law, Steve, is a GP in London and he said from the offset that her problem was neurological, but the consultants in Wythenshawe disagreed with him. He was right however, because after nine weeks we were told that Mum was terminally ill, suffering from multi-system atrophy. Mum died in hospital on her own, the night following the meeting that was held in hospital to arrange her discharge. Mum was to come and live with us; her fear had always been that she would have to go and live in a nursing home some day and I was determined that this could not happen to her. Sadly, she did not pass peacefully.

I felt great anger at how she had been treated – the lack of respect shown to her was crippling. In all those weeks, only four staff were kind to her. She had her teeth cleaned only three times in all the time spent in that hospital. It was a task she could no longer do by herself due to her failing health – but she did not tell me this until the day she died. This seemed so sad to me. That she could not complete such a mundane task was a huge loss of dignity for a lady who was very independent and proud. Most staff treated her as a burden and even worse, a hypochondriac: the head physiotherapist claimed that she was putting on the falling over as she did not want to come and live with me! They were so wrong though and the thing that gives me peace is that we were there for Mum. We created space and a bathroom for her in our home. She knew she was loved. The poor care was not the reason for her death and it could not have been prevented, but my regret is that she should have been at home with us, not in that soulless institution.

ERIC AND PRIMARY SCHOOL

Eric loved Mum and when she died, his devastation was massive. Their relationship was unique and, from day one, they bonded: he chatted, she chatted, they were best friends. She called herself his 'bench' because as she was sitting on the sofa – or indeed sitting anywhere – he would plonk himself into her lap for a hug, for contact. Mum was never too busy for him. I think that in some ways, Eric replaced Mum's stillborn son, who she lost many years ago, and who would have been our older brother.

The gap left by my Mum was too big for Eric to bear and his behaviour became worse. I asked for extra support from school, but they refused, saying that there was no money in the budget. After many visits to school, often led by a complaint about Eric, I managed to secure a small amount of additional support through the behaviour team. This help was impeded by the fact that the person providing the support and advice had somehow upset the Head, meaning she was out of favour and, therefore, was not listened to.

This support should have been for eight weeks and then the school should have taken over responsibility, but they refused – I have never really understood why, as it was obvious that the teachers were not coping with him. However, the support from the behaviour team continued throughout Year 6 and they "mopped up" when the school failed to help. Eric spent most of his time being sent out of class, being bullied by the other children, being excluded, and, it has to be said, being bullied by the staff.

Every incident was blamed upon him and consequently, his behaviour worsened. As I've stated before, I was constantly told about his behaviour issues in front of him, but I insisted that he should leave whilst they admonished me, shamed me. I said to one teacher, "You are shaming him by going through all his bad behaviours in front of him" – and this was not the first time I had this conversation – but she looked at me as if I was talking another language. There was never a change in how they dealt with him – it was as if they expected me to be able manage his behaviour for them, even though I was at home. There was never a sense of collaboration, yet this continuity between home and school is something that an attachment disordered children needs to feel safe.

Getting into school was always a challenge. Getting up, getting dressed, getting out of the door all presented numerous opportunities to evoke rage. Most of the time, I had to hold onto Eric in order to get him up the high street without him running into the road. This was not a pretty sight, for I had to grab on to whatever part of him I could as he would not hold my hand calmly. I always wondered what people thought as they drove past, calm and collected in their metal boxes. We both arrived, purposely just as the bell went, in an angry, upset heap. The one concession made for us in Year 6 was for him to arrive 10 minutes early for one-to-one time, but this was not one-to-one at all really as the teachers were just gearing up for the day. He hated going in early and sometimes ran off from me. He wanted to play with the other boys, but they just wanted to wind him up. They played in a way that isolated him, a fact nobody addressed. For example, in order to fit in, Eric started to "act out" towards the boy he saw as being the most popular. He would try and engage with them in all the wrong ways and they saw him as easy meat: easy to provoke, easy to leave out and easy to ridicule. It was cruel. He started a pattern of "serial head-butting", in that his way of becoming friends was to taunt the toughest boy until he hit out at Eric. He hated to be hit, but would laugh like a maniac, as if he had won something. The pattern would then repeat – and has done so ever since.

I requested an Educational Psychologist report in Year 5 – but the school forgot to put in the form. I requested it again, a year later, in the June of Year 6, and he was assessed. The EP, Sue Hawkins, was great. She understood attachment. She understood Eric. The problem was, it was too late for his primary school. She recommended a Statement, but the primary school had, in effect, already washed their hands of him. Nothing was submitted and, in their eyes, it was now down to the secondary school to action the assessment.

7

ERIC AND SECONDARY SCHOOL

When Eric entered secondary school, they did not action the recommendations until they had to, which meant that more precious months were lost. We had high hopes for Kingsway High School because we had spent a number of hours with them going through Eric's needs – specifically, the need for a secure adult to supervise him. Copious notes were made and we really hoped that the transition would be smooth. We were experts in our traumatised child and we knew that any transition for Eric was never going to be easy.

By Eric's second day at the new school, I was already alarmed. The promises that had been made about extra support being available to help with the change were not met, the excuse being that the Year 7s were "off timetable" – a weak excuse, if ever I've heard one. By week two, we were in the Head's office, and it seemed all the work we had done – about the whole essence of an attachment disordered child – had apparently been lost in translation. We explained what he needed and the consequences if these needs were not met in that his behaviour had already begun to 'spiral' and, if not caught early, would gather momentum. He needed a secure base, a secure adult and to feel safe. At the moment, he did not feel safe.

In an effort to guarantee the best transition possible for Eric, we met with the Head and Deputy Head on a number of occasions. The Deputy Head said that, even with a Statement, Eric would not get any extra hours of specialist support and that the only reason he had any additional hours now was because we were "complaining". The SENCO at this new school was clueless and very rude – very "old school" – for example, she sat in one meeting, slouched down in her chair with her arms crossed. Her body language said it all: it was obvious that she was not minded to help Eric.

Things were not great, but, eventually, he did have some additional hours allocated to him. The SENCO gave me a timetable that was hard to understand, but claimed that he now had 16 hours of additional help. When this was broken down, the majority was Learning Support Assistant hours that were used collectively for a class of approximately 30 students. Eric was also allocated 20 minutes in the morning to connect with someone from the student support area, but, unfortunately, the person allocated dropped her daughter off first, leaving him with about 10 minutes, during which he had to get to his first class.

The secondary school was massive, with 1500 children spread over two sites, separated by a subway. Using the subway terrified Eric because it was where he often got hit and pushed and he generally felt threatened there. The suggested solution was for him to go back to the Support Centre and get escorted to his next lesson, but there was a fundamental flaw in the logic: getting to the Support Centre meant navigating the subway and all that this entailed.

We pushed at the Council and the school for the Statement to be expedited because Eric was in meltdown and we felt that it would help him. Every day, he was being hit, kicked and bullied – and he was not coping because there was no secure adult for him to turn to. Nobody except for his two older sisters were looking out for him at school. Zoe ended up getting punched in the face trying to protect him and, in fact, they were both suffering because of his behaviour. They were "picked on" because of Eric, but, whilst they were embarrassed, they were also very loyal to him. In the end, we realised that Kingsway could not support him and keep him safe.

I rang the EP (Sue Hawkins), who had assessed him in Year 6 and she suggested a special school, with smaller class sizes and specialist teachers. At first, I was devastated because I wanted a normal school for him and didn't want for him to be stigmatised further, but this EP was the only person who gave clear advice based on HIS needs.

We listened, looked at the school she recommended and I suspended my aversion to special schools and fought to get him a place there. He was threatening suicide by this time and was desperate and unhappy. We succeeded in getting the Statement through quickly, it has to be said, by making ourselves very unpopular with the people in the Education Department and Eric was allocated 25 hours support. The Deputy Head, however, did not apologise for the lack of support we received.

Thankfully, by February half-term, Eric was in his new school and, by his May report, he had achieved the most merits for Year 7. The staff found him to be a real character – he was making friends, managing to learn to walk away from conflict and to stop interfering so much. Eric said he loved his new school, but this did not last.

8

SHAME

The Oxford English Dictionary (2013, p.838) defines "shame" as, "A painful feeling of embarrassment or distress arising from being aware that you have done something wrong or foolish: (2). A loss of respect".

A sense of shame is commonplace in the life of adopters and adopted alike. Individuals who are adopted often develop attachment issues because there is a fracture in their sense of self due to being taken away from their birth parents. With attachment disorders comes a great sense of overpowering, all-encompassing shame.

Shame is a deep emotion. It starts at the very core of a person and spreads through the body on a visceral level. It is that feeling you may have experienced when you were younger and are told off by a teacher/adult/parent in a very parent/child manner (the Transactional Analysis model). That feeling of going red with embarrassment, the worry about what people think of you, the shame of being "caught out".

This emotion is deeply rooted in many adopted children. Fundamentally, they feel that they were adopted because of their flaws: that they were not good enough, that they were bad. Many interactions in their life will take them right back to these early emotions and feelings of complete worthlessness, feelings of having nothing of value to contribute, nothing left to lose. Shame is based on being the one in the wrong, being powerless and embarrassed. For child and parent alike, shame has a parallel process.

For adopters and adoptees alike, attachment disorder is not easy to deal with. Equally, schools do not cope well with disruptive students and fellow pupils see weaknesses and opportunities to bully in equal measure. The fall out of this is that, as parents, you are constantly required to do the "walk of shame" in the playground, where – as I have detailed previously – teachers seem to take great delight in regaling you with your son/daughter's misdemeanours. The shame of the given situation is felt both by your charge and directly by you and you are often seen as an ineffectual or a bad parent. The adoptive parent feels this shame vicariously.

An example of this is when a Year 6 teacher summoned us at the end of the school day and gave Eric a dressing-down because he'd refused to move when sitting in the school hall. I asked Eric to leave the room, then asked her to try and empathise with how this shaming was for

Eric, but she was clueless, even when I described exactly how he felt! After this particular event, Eric ran off from me and I couldn't find him. His sense of shame was so great that he could not stay in our vicinity. After some anxiety, I found him hiding in the school yard and he was expecting me be angry with him too. I just put my arm around him and said how hard he must find things at school – just being Eric. The floodgates opened and he sobbed his heart out.

I have been summoned to school so many times for similar dressing-downs. Amazingly, when it suits the teacher, they can see me immediately – no appointment necessary. I asked them to ring me and I would come in before school, after school, at lunchtime or PPA time – but, no, I was always chastised at a time suitable to them, with no prior warning of the incident, which meant I was always on the back foot, being told off and having to think in the moment, whereas they were prepared and had all the facts, such as they were.

On the other hand, when I requested to see them, they couldn't see me sometimes until the following week – and I knew this was because they needed time to prepare. I feel that as a parent of a complex child, help for a child often has to be fought for – it is not always freely given. This requires the parent – in this case, me – to assume a challenging role that is often very uncomfortable for all concerned. Teachers are experts in teaching, but parents know their child and this can be perceived as criticism, especially when resources are scarce, but the needs of many students remain high. Review meetings were the same, of which there were many – but not quite enough to meet the criteria for additional support. I always asked for a copy of all reports before meetings, but this courtesy was not afforded to me. I went into every meeting, blind, outnumbered and unprepared. They held all the power, the reports and the opinions and we, as parents, had to sit, as if in the naughty chair, surrounded by a number of often clueless "professionals" (always after being told how busy they were and that the meeting could only go on for 10 minutes, I might add). They read and tried to assimilate the reports and interpret the jargon – anything to hide the fact that they had nothing of import to say. If nothing is said, nothing is measurable, nothing and nobody is accountable.

At Eric's secondary school, the same responses and actions continued. It was institutionalisation at its worst. Everyone was always far too busy to meet and the mantra was, "Just sign the form". Asking for details was a crime too far: "Who are all these people supporting Eric? For how many hours? How come he has never seen them or doesn't know them?" All my queries were met defensively: "Just sign the forms, please."

Every child with additional needs requires a plan that tracks their needs and achievements, but they must be SMART goals or else how can progress be measured? The plan for Eric at Kingsway was vague and non-specific, so much so that it was not useful at all. I asked for the goals to be clearly defined, only to be met with blank stares. *Measurable, Mrs. Morrissey? I think not! Time-bound? I think not. In fact, we shall just regurgitate all the same goals, year in, year out?*

My attempts to explain behavioural management to teaching staff were met with superior looks, blank eyes, set mouths – as if I was talking gobbledygook. They were so condescending, viewing me as the "poor parent" trying to tell them how to deal with these children. Any explanation about my relevant background in the police, with Mencap and as a counsellor was met with little interest. It was if there was an unspoken rule: *Always treat the parent as the "mad woman in the attic" and you can't go far wrong.* The feeling I was left with was one of shame: shame at being unsuccessful in my efforts to improve Eric's school experience; shame at being seen as a bad parent and, therefore, a bad person.

So, shame is my world and I regularly have feelings of humiliation and distress – engendered by being *made* to feel wrong and foolish by others – although in actuality, I know that my actions are not wrong and neither are they foolish. I have to keep reminding myself and Eric of this fact – nonetheless, this "shame setting" in our psyche is now ingrained, easily triggered and deeply rooted.

Each negative comment made about our child (or us) is taken on board at this instinctive level of being wrong, foolish. The shame faced on campsites when our child is rude or swears, or when an angry parent comes to tell us of the sins of our child, never diminishes, even though we know that Eric struggles so much, every day of his life.

SHAME

Recently, I met with a lovely lady, the mother of one of Eric's few friends. Prior to this meeting, I'd had to rearrange a trip to the BMX track with her son at short notice due to Eric's bad behaviour. Eric, of course, was raging and I was upset. We met up for the boys to play football whilst we had coffee in the café. After a while, she said to me, "Please don't cancel like that again – my son was devastated." I was disappointed at her reaction because, as a mother, I hoped she'd have some awareness of my predicament. What was I supposed to do? I'm sorry her son was upset, but my son was aggressive, rude and raging at me, so how could I reward him for that behaviour with a trip to the BMX track? I told her that I didn't want to cancel and that I try never to let people down, but, in this case, I felt I had no choice. I ended up trying to explain my life and Eric's complexities in detail, in an effort to get her to understand that my actions are never taken lightly and are never meant to harm others.

I'm not entirely sure if she understood my dilemma though and, inevitably, I ended up feeling in the wrong. It demonstrated that even the most well-meaning people do not really understand another's circumstances. Her son is calm and well-behaved and I think she sees the fact that my son isn't either of those things as somehow my fault.

Trying to explain the depths we can descend to in our family life feels shameful and sad. I think that unless you have been there, you can never truly appreciate the shame, the sadness, the despair and, yes, the disappointment in how judgemental the world is, how unforgiving. I have never, nor do I intend to, enlighten parents about their offspring's shortcomings. Why would I? Do they really need to hear it? What purpose does it serve? Who is benefitting? Asking for help is one thing – however, not asking, but always being given unsolicited advice, just compounds a traumatic situation and heaps on the shame – whilst, at the same time, it highlights how narrow people's views of the world actually are – the very inability to walk in another's shoes is a limiting factor in many lives, I feel. I, perhaps, have developed too much empathy, the weight of which can be crippling.

How to heal the "shamed" individual

In order to recover, the individual needs to move from the feeling of shame to a feeling of self-worth. This can be an incredibly slow, tortuous process and requires a gentle approach that heals with kindness and understanding.

Shame is like a battle scar. To see it for what it is, to see where it comes from and to accept it, is the start of a journey to integrate the feelings acquired through a life affected by trauma.

Self-acceptance – flaws and all – helps an individual love themselves. This assists in their attachment to others and to groups because they find it easier to integrate if they like themselves first and foremost. Integration and acceptance then help the feelings of shame to fade. It is no longer the "go to" emotion.

To start the healing process, the individual must feel accepted for who they are. In a school setting, this begins when a teacher "gets" the child. They just naturally have empathy for them, take the time to know them and provide a secure base. When things go awry, they talk things through, without attributing blame, but seek other solutions. The child is less upset, feels calmer and creates fewer opportunities to get things wrong. The shamed child needs to feel valued and to have their successes recognised, rather than their failings. The things that they excel at need to be highlighted. Each positive response is like a penny being added to an empty jar.

The parent will heal when their child is accepted and the cup flows over when the ostracised child gains friends, as this is a true mark of progress. To be heard by professionals and credited with skills previously overlooked is healing in itself, so child and parent heal in a parallel process.

Therapeutically, the shamed individual can start to heal because they have a voice and can understand their life from new perspectives. The therapist acts as the secure base of acceptance until they are sufficiently healed to provide this foundation for themselves. In all of the above cases, Lifespan Integration Therapy can heal wounds that are acknowledged and those that are somatically (body-held) and hover beneath the consciousness of the individual. Time is a great healer and this is a truth, but only if the shaming of the child or parent stops. The greatest gift a professional can give a shamed person is their respect, their time and most importantly an apology for hurts delivered wittingly or unwittingly upon the psyche of the individual.

9

THE SITUATION AT HOME

Home has always been where all the wars are fought. From getting up time to bedtime, conflict abounds. My mood is determined by Eric, as is the case with the rest of the family, for if he is in an angry mood, this affects us all. He will pick a fight and argue about nothing at all until everyone is cross and exasperated. His aggression knows no limits. He loves to slam doors really hard, kick at things, including my dogs, myself and the girls. He will throw whatever is at hand and hit out at us. Eric is rude and aggressive when Dermot is around, but also views him with caution and, although I am loathe to admit it, with a little more respect. When Derm was on afternoon or night shifts, Eric would get a glint in his eye and it would be "game on", as he knew that it was harder for me to navigate his tantrums on my own – partially because I could not just leave him at home on his own if was refusing to come with me when I needed to get something or take the girls somewhere.

The worse things are at school, the worse the situation is at home. I have had to barricade him in his room, with me in front of the door to stop him coming out, whilst he rages and trashes his room. I try and read to remain calm, which is somewhat challenging when items of electronic gadgetry are flying at the door.

Eric will refuse all requests, such as, "Please eat your breakfast/make your lunch/clean your teeth/have a shower/put your shoes on/pick that up …" He hates to help with any tasks and retorts, "You do it!" Bargaining and incentives fail miserably. I always stick to threatened punishments, but they have little or no affect.

Our house is a maelstrom of stress, anger and anxiety and I am the lightning rod for all his angst. As the primary carer – and, therefore, the rule-maker – I cause his angst through my requests and decision-making, but I am also the only real solution to it too. As he goes through puberty, he is becoming taller and stronger – he is much taller than me now – and I wonder how I will manage him as he grows. He gets so annoyed that common sense leaves him altogether. He often threatens to run away and will cross roads without looking and he has even been known to plant himself in the middle of a road as an act of defiance. Yet, when he is calm, he is funny, loving and full of a natural empathy for others. The trick is to find the calm. I believe Eric to be bright and he has a phenomenal memory, especially about football! He can talk to any adult and beguile them with his personality and humour. He loves us all, but I am his special bond, always there, loving him and protecting him. This, I feel he knows on a deep level. We have a special, immensely strong bond that all the tears have never broken – in fact, they have probably acted like glue, joining us together.

Holidays

Our holidays are not as the rest of the population might experience them! We take our ball of stress with us and, coupled with the fact that Eric gets stressed with any change, holidays are fraught with tension which impacts on the lead up to them, the journey, the first few days, the return and re-acclimatisation to home.

On top of this is the issue of socially "getting it wrong". Due to his issues, Eric wants to play with others, but lacks the ability to do so. He charges in and tries to control all games and events, which doesn't go down so well. In a nutshell, he is the child who no one wants to play with. All I can hear is his loud voice shrieking in the wind, about how he has been wronged or left out or hit. I sit in dread when he goes off exploring the campsite: I have my shoulders up around my ears, waiting for the inevitable tantrum or for another child to come complaining about him or worse still, an irate father banging on the caravan door with some complaint or other.

When adults get involved in their children's rivalries, I find it very strange. I am yet to accost another parent to complain about their child. If things go wrong, I suggest that they stay away from the situation and allow things to pass, yet in my experience, parents love to just let you know that your child is doing this or that … Most of the time, I don't need to know – in fact it would be kinder not to share this information with me at all!

Support networks

One of our main support networks, MAS (Manchester Adoption Society) was funded through charitable funding, but sadly they had to close down and our case was not transferred or picked up by the local council. When MAS disappeared, so did that particular lifeline. However, we had been referred to Mary Kelsall, a Child Psychiatrist at Pendlebury Children's Hospital through MAS. She was very supportive and reassured us that we were doing all the right things. She told us we were being "therapeutic parents" which was good to know. Shortly after Mum died, I contacted Mary, but it was clear after we'd spoken that we were no longer on her books. Public funding cuts were already taking their toll on her services.

I felt that that door was firmly, if sympathetically, shut behind me, too.

I could have – in retrospect, perhaps I should have – made contact with Stockport Social Services, but, if truth be told, I was so exhausted that I didn't have the energy: it all seemed too much effort. I have looked at their website many times and been met with generic e-mail contact forms, mainly focused on becoming a foster carer for Stockport, which just didn't relate to my circumstances in any way. There were no human faces or names of people I could speak to – it was yet another bureaucratic, faceless machine. Since embarking on the adoption path, my faith in "professional" bodies such as these has been sorely tested.

I have always had a good set of friends, but the ones I met when Eric was in nursery had fallen by the wayside: some just drifted, most just did not really get Eric. Or, when they sailed off back into the workplace, I was left in their wake, no longer useful as the friend to have coffee with when they were at a loose end. My friendship had a shelf life. Other long-standing friendships are still there, but work and distance create barriers.

After my mum died, I realised how much she'd given me in terms of friendship, support and company. We did not always get it right and we argued as any mum and daughter might. Mum was not one for flowery praise, but when we were out together for lunch or coffee, she would look at me with her wise blue eyes, and say what a good mum I was – and I believed her. She shored me up and made me believe that I could do it – I could parent Eric. Mum always said that she could see us in the future, with Eric towering over me, his arm around me, looking after me. She told me that my relationship with Eric would solidify over time and become inviolable. Mum gave me hope for the future.

My sister is great. She actively tries to fill the void left by Mum's passing, but she lives in London. We spend as much time together as possible, but it is not a "just around the corner" relationship sadly for both of us.

So, in terms of support, it's fair to say that there wasn't much of it around for me and my family. At one point, I came across the Adoption Research Institute (ARI) and I thought it was just what I needed. However, I was disappointed to see that the research around support was aimed predominantly at support for the birth families and for continued contact – not for the adoptive families.

Dermot

My husband! He is a great partner and dad, but, unfortunately, he has been a police officer for 30 years, retiring just over a year ago. I say "unfortunately" about being in the police because he hated it. It was the wrong career choice for a musical, kind-hearted man. He grew up in Belfast through The Troubles, a bleak time in its history. It was

THE SITUATION AT HOME

a war zone – Catholics killing Protestants, Protestants killing Catholics – with no end in sight. In the middle of this, Dermot was one of six children, the family living on a policeman's wage, which at that time was barely a living wage. Additionally, his dad was a Catholic in a Protestant organisation. His dad saw things that he should not have seen; he lived when friends had died. His mum suffered also, living in constant fear: would her husband make it home that night?

Derm went to university, studying languages, but his main love was music. He played in a rock band and wanted to become a rock star. Instead, after two years on the dole, applying unsuccessfully for jobs in a climate of scarce work opportunities, whilst playing in the band, his dad delivered an ultimatum. Apply for the Royal Ulster Constabulary (form in hand) or leave home. Derm did leave home, but, ironically, joined the Greater Manchester Police instead. He struggled with the mentality of the police in the UK, coming from a war zone where life and death was a daily occurrence, to Salford where the priorities were whether or not your vehicle had road tax. His first two years were harsh as he struggled to adapt.

The early years in the police force affected his confidence. He did achieve the rank of inspector, but served most of his time doing shift work, resulting in acute tiredness, a bad temper and non-stop migraines. His lack of self-belief prevented him from applying for the CID or different squads, so he stuck with what he knew, although he was a far better police officer than he ever believed. He had a photographic memory for faces and an ability to talk to anyone – he also ran faster than any criminal could! For a period of about four years, he also suffered from debilitating depression, the depth of which I was unable to acknowledge at the time. Living with depression is isolating, lonely and frightening for him, but also for me. I wondered whether he was ever going to "come back" to us. Thankfully, he did come back.

The hardest thing as a family, with a parent on shift work, is the fact that Dermot would be working three weekends out of five. At a time when exposure to Eric was at its most intensive due to there being no schooling, I was on my own. This took its toll: Eric would ask what shift his dad was on, and, if it was the afternoon shift, he would get a glint in his eye, as if to say, "Game on!" This meant major tantrums, pushing, screaming and a complete refusal to comply. There was no time for recuperation because, as the sun set on the Sunday, so the school week loomed and the anxiety ratcheted up.

Friends disappeared into their calm family units at weekends and, especially over the last year of Derm being in the police, I was increasingly on my own all weekend. Eric was and still is unable to enter into out of school activities. Due to his social issues, he just antagonises others and comes home feeling an acute sense of shame and failure, which is communicated via foul behaviour and language. He needed to spread his wings, but sadly the world was not ready for him. This meant that myself and the girls were confined to home as Eric refused to join in with us in whatever we wanted to do. He could not be left on his own, so we all stayed put, wings clipped. He does not have friends as such and he does not, nor has he ever had, sleepovers. He does not have birthday parties anymore because who would come? He would just get completely stressed and angry. He does not get invited to parties either – even friends of ours who have a child a year younger than Eric and who used to come to our house for Eric's birthday, stopped inviting Eric to their son's football parties about two years ago. I feel so sad for Eric, I could cry for him, and all of this increases his feeling of isolation.

Dermot retired in June 2015 and I worried that he would struggle adapting to life at home – but I was wrong! His migraines increased, however, until in the summer of 2016, he actually attended a physiotherapist to help with them and had acupuncture. He was then advised to come off all medication and, for the first time in years, his migraines subsided. The new dynamic in our household eventually settled, but Derm's retirement saw a horrendous spike in Eric's behaviour, partly I feel because he could no longer bully me and the girls. He could not fight both of us all the time and we could begin to divide and rule, in that if one child needed to go to jujitsu for example, I could take her and Derm could stay at home with Eric if he refused to come. This in itself would mean that conflict could be avoided rather than managed.

My future career prospects

Another effect of adopting a child with attachment issues is the impact it can have on the carer's working life. I always worked prior to having my family and intended to return to work, but there was no way I could've imagined what obstacles lay ahead for me in this respect. The first, of course, being Eric: he needs me to see him off to school in the mornings and he needs me there when he returns home. He needs me to be available at all times. The school also expects me to be there at the drop of a hat, ready to attend numerous meetings. CAMHS, Social Services and any number of other professionals always set up meetings in school hours, which means for me to return to employment and get to all the meetings would never have worked.

The second factor is school holidays. I have no family networks to help out and Eric cannot access "normal" holiday provision because he needs specific support and does not, in all honesty, want to join in these groups as he finds relationships with his peers so complex. Thus, my working life would have to mirror the school day and be in term time only. Not many jobs would be able to accommodate me.

The third factor is that I have now been out of the workplace since 2001. I still feel that I could do any managerial job, but I doubt that employers would be willing to take that risk. This is a common dilemma for people who step out of the workplace to bring up their children. I also realised that I had, over the years, learnt a lot of invaluable lessons that I wanted to share with others and that I needed a focus for my energy.

I realise that I am a "therapeutic parent", in that I have a thirst for knowledge and a drive to find new ways of dealing with my son's attachment issues. This quest for knowledge led me into counselling because it was a natural extension of my home life and previous occupations, using my knowledge in a positive way. The police force teaches communication, no matter the background. To be a good police officer requires insight and adaptability. My work for people with learning disabilities taught me about being truly person-centred – and the yard stick of, 'Would this be good enough for my mother/brother/daughter?' is one that I permanently hold in front of me, whatever I do.

I decided that becoming qualified as a counsellor was a calling for me, a natural path for me to pursue. It would put my knowledge and experience to good use and give me a sense of direction. I trained and set up my own private practice, managing to secure work in a local sixth form and a secondary school. I was able to be my own boss, an objective that had been spurring me on for quite some time. After accreditation, I have continued to learn and seek knowledge, whilst maintaining my interest in attachment and trauma. The road led me to train in Lifespan Integration Therapy, a therapy that heals trauma and attachment, whereas previously it was believed that attachment disorders were recognisable, but not treatable. This I find amazing and it holds true hope for the future of so many individuals. I am excited about the direction my life is taking.

10

THE CHANGING FACE OF ADOPTION

Adoption has radically altered over recent years. No longer is the shamed young girl forced into having her baby adopted against her will. This, of course, can still happen, but the societal taboo of single motherhood is no longer the same. Society has evolved to the point where unwanted pregnancies are easily prevented via birth control, morning after pills or abortion. Pregnancy is now continued through to birth largely through choice. Often, for young mothers, the promise of an escape from a difficult home life can be motivation enough to keep the baby, if even it is not really wanted, although this is likely to lead to problems further down the line.

Children are rarely "given up" for adoption. They are more likely to be taken from their birth parents after having been subjected to abuse and/or neglect. Adoptions are rarely voluntary or planned. This means that trauma and neglect permeates the lives of these children, whilst the system designed to save them slowly trundles on. Often it is too little, too late.

It seems that the older siblings are the "sacrificial lambs" in the experiment of inadequate parenting. Once, this experiment in parenthood fails, the younger siblings may well be "rescued", but for the older children, the damage has been done – and they're all likely to suffer from attachment disorder. The pre-adoption environment invariably sets up the child to be traumatised, but, even so, to remove children from birth parents should never be taken lightly because every act of removal causes trauma. However, as with all things, a balance needs to be struck. If a parent is unable to meet the demands presented by rearing a child, then this decision needs to be expedited.

In Eric's case, his six older siblings were all adopted and his mother was imprisoned because of child neglect, so the writing was on the wall for Eric as his birth mother would not ever be able to safely parent a child. And yet Eric languished in poor foster care for nearly two-and-a-half years, having been removed from her at birth. It was this avoidable delay that did the most harm to my son. The decision that a child needs to be removed from his/her birth parents needs to be thoroughly assessed, but with urgency. Then the placement with an adoptive family must be done with as little delay as possible.

The Department for Education and Skills commissioned the Adoption Research Initiative (ARI) to evaluate the Adoption and Children Act 2002 (2013: Thomas), along with other related the policy initiatives, which aimed to:

- Improve planning for permanence for looked-after children and increase the number of children who are adopted
- Reduce delay in the relevant social work and court processes
- Improve adoption services, particularly support services
- Put the needs and rights of the child at the centre of the adoption process

Research has shown that the younger the child, the better the likely outcome for adoption placements. This "success" is also determined by the stability and resilience of the carers. Some foster carers were reluctant to adopt purely because they felt that support would then end because, once a court rules for the adoption, the responsibility of Social Services ends. The Adoption and Children Act (2002) introduced Special Guardianship Orders (SGO) as a further option when planning permanent solutions, where adoption is not an appropriate solution.

The study identified the key messages, one of which being that many of the special guardians were grandparents and, therefore, ageing. Provision was needed to plan for future issues created by elderly carers, a need to provide appropriate support and adequate projected funding to support delivery of care. These factors, I would argue, would positively impact on all permanency provision planning, not just for SGOs.

I attempted to contact people involved in the research and was met with silence and a feeling of, "Get back in your box" from the professor involved in the research into permanency and adoption. They had moved onto another area of research and could not inform me as to how, or, indeed, if it was to be rolled out. This image of important scholastic treaties gathering dust is very depressing. The research was funded, but it was then shelved. What is the point of research, if we are not informed as to how it is to be implemented or, indeed, if it is to be implemented?

Meanwhile, adopting children from overseas countries has flourished, despite some catastrophes. This kind of adoption has its own unique set of problems. Attachment issues are common, alongside a loss of cultural identity. If people adopt from other races, the differences are apparent for all to see. The adoptee is always reminded that they are different from their parents and everyone will know immediately that they have an "interesting" history. There is the additional obligation, I believe, to honour their birth culture and learn their cultural ways, so that the adopted child has a sense of self, of belonging.

The potentially greatest changes in adoption though are through the development of the Regional Adoption Agencies (RAA). In May 2015, the government announced that by 2020 adoption services should be delivered on a regional basis, with the objective of becoming more effective, efficient and at the same time, reducing the number of adoption agencies. The aim is to increase the numbers of children being adopted and, at the same time, reduce the length of time a child is left waiting to be adopted. The purpose of the RAAs is also to improve post-adoption support. The RAAs could be a really positive change in the world of adoption, as long as new initiatives are encouraged. As with all change, the process can be cumbersome, but if the objectives are truly achieved, then adoptees and adopters alike could feel the impact.

The repercussions of adoption

In the main, adopters go into adoption believing that love can heal a child, but the premise that love conquers all is not the whole truth. Love and acceptance and a big heart are essential qualities in adoptive parents, but love is not always enough to heal the wounds. Nonetheless, many people want a family and, for whatever reason – be it infertility, the lack of a suitable partner or the desire to give a child a home – they opt to adopt. I've heard it said in Social Services circles that adoption is not about the adopters having a child, but about the child having a family. I disagree. Both parties are of equal import and should be treated as such.

When a child is adopted, they are traumatised on some level. They will always have "lost" a part of themselves. Add into the mix, the neglect, abuse and pain that some young people/children endure and love is not enough. The adoptive parents must become therapeutic parents. They must learn and understand the loss that has been endured, the issues this can create and work out how to support the wounded child. The possible effects of adoption are lifelong, so both the parents and children must become resilient. The wounds of the child become the wounds of the adoptive parents and they are bound together by pain at times.

Birth families do not just disappear either. They are forever hovering on the periphery of the adoptee's consciousness. Questions are raised about birth family members that it may not be possible to answer: "Are they still alive, are they okay, why can't I see them?" Adopters often feel that they should be enough, but the reality is that they are often not enough and this can be wounding. With adoption comes the increased awareness that, as with all children, but especially with adopted children, they are on loan. They may well opt to return to the birth family when they are older. Years of love, of tears, may still be met with loss. Birth parents can also face this, obviously, but, with adoption, there is always a ready-made alternative waiting in the wings.

Social media has made this potential source of connection for adoptee teens an ever-present reality. There are also massive search engines at their fingertips, pumping out information and knowledge. They can search and locate family members from the privacy of their room, connected to the Internet at all times.

Access to birth families is no longer the right of adoptive parents or Social Services to grant. The adoptee can do it for themselves. The issue with this is that birth parents are rarely the prince and princesses dreamt up by the wounded child. Mainly, they have been removed for very good reason, but, in their childish imaginations, the adoptees will embroider an elaborate alternate reality that paints their birthparents as heroes.

The issue is that the freedom to search the Internet can uncover devastating truths that are hard to bear. Recently, my middle daughter connected with her older brother who lives in the northeast of England. He had tried to commit suicide and written about it on Facebook. My daughter was on a residential course with the National Citizens Service (NCS) at the time and I had a call at 11pm to say that she was distraught. I had to calm her down and then ring the Darlington Social Services to ensure that her brother was being kept safe. They were very unhelpful, saying that it was not their problem and that I should ring the police. I refused as I knew nothing of his personal details – details that I knew they would have access to.

My daughter has also been in contact with her birth father on Facebook, even though we said not to. The issue here is that the contact is not supported and they are not prepared for the aftershocks of this exposure. Previously, adoptees had to go through Social Services and had input on resilience and expectations – in other words, support before and after the reconnection. Now adoptees head off on their own and may not seek help if things become painful.

A more important issue with this freedom of information is that if the child has been removed because of abuse, they can still contact or be contacted and traced by their abusers: they cannot hide, they have no anonymity. There are no measures in place to keep these vulnerable children safe. I think that this is a minefield for the future of adoption.

11

TRAUMA AND SECONDARY TRAUMA

Trauma is an emotional response to a terrible event … Immediately after the event, shock and denial are typical. Longer term reactions include unpredictable emotions, flashbacks, strained relationships and even physical symptoms like headaches or nausea. While these feelings are normal, some people have difficulty moving on with their lives.

—American Psychological Association

Trauma overwhelms the individual, preventing them from moving on in their life; they are stuck in the past, reliving the events, consciously or unconsciously. The traumatic event damages the individual psyche, creating feelings of anxiety, being driven and out of control. Just being born can create trauma, but to be adopted is a trauma on a primal level. The event exists somatically (in the body), if not in the narrative, of the individual affected. They know that something is wrong, but do not know what or why they feel as they do.

This trauma is often undiagnosed or therapeutically unmanaged. Children proceed into adulthood through the foster care systems or through adoption without receiving therapy. Often they display signs of having PTSD (Post Traumatic Stress Disorder) that affects their ability to feel safe, to bond with others or build secure adult relationships. This trauma is often displayed in very anti-social behaviour that can be both withdrawn and aggressive. The adopted child projects these feelings of insecurity and fear on their adoptive families and others that they come into contact with.

Secondary trauma

I have lived a life affected by secondary attachment trauma. The trauma of losing his birth mother and then his subsequent neglect whilst in foster care means that Eric is traumatised and his anger and grief found a lightning rod in me. His pain was fired at me on a daily basis and his trauma became my trauma. I suffered alongside him.

This path, unwittingly trod, started when I adopted my Eric. I had not previously heard of secondary trauma, but in my search to understand the daily issues I was dealing with, I became interested in trauma and attachment. To me, the two are interlinked. It took me a while longer to connect how I was feeling with the fact that I was a sufferer of secondary trauma.

I suppose that I was in denial. I had always been the "coper", the doer – Mum even called me "Old Mother Hubbard" because I was the one who helped everyone else. When I was younger, I felt there was nothing that my strength of will could not overcome. On reflection, this was probably my undoing. I did not know how to fall gracefully, how to ask for help, for understanding – instead, I soldiered on until I hit a wall.

The wall was very unforgiving and the collision happened due to an accumulation of many tiny – and not so tiny – cuts over the past 10 years: each incident at school, each issue with other parents adding to the load I was carrying. The death of my mum took my feet from under me, but still I forged on. I fought the system as bureaucracy is not tolerated by someone like me! I never have accepted the simple, complacent answer of "No", because it is often based purely on apathy and a lack of imagination, a culture that large public sector organisations breed.

I hate rules that don't make sense. I hate people who hide behind regulations and excuse poor or cruel behaviour on spending cuts or the pressure of work. I believe that, whilst we cannot take on the global economy, we can have an impact on those in our circles of influence. The wider ramifications do not excuse an inhuman treatment of others.

To fight the educational system on behalf of Eric was awful. I felt like a wind-up mouse, constantly head-butting a concrete wall. I would be floored, get up and start again. To give up was not an option because he deserved better. The irony was that I was battling for something that I fundamentally disagreed with because I was fighting for a Statement of Special Educational Needs and I have never liked labels: a person is not an epileptic, they have epilepsy. No person should be defined by an illness or disability and to define them in these terms limits their aspirations and their dreams.

However, in order to get Eric the support he needed, I had to bite the bullet. I was unable to change an archaic system. I felt that the teachers should have a Statement or at the very least they should be challenged on their poor practice. They should be educated on how to manage behaviourally challenging children, equipped with a toolbox of approaches that could meet the children's needs. The tide could be reversed with accountability or at least a desire to do their job better so that children in this category could be saved from the scrap heap.

At present the "system" meets challenging behaviour head on. It isolates, punishes, excludes and expels and, during this, the young people involved are not learning. They will leave 15 years of education without a qualification to their name. Certainly that is where Eric was headed.

My training to become a counsellor was sparked by a desire to help others who were going through similar struggles to me, who were experiencing things from their side of the "war". War is a strong word, but, at times, that it what the battle felt like: a war of raging hurt, pain and fear and the target is the person who is left standing the longest – the one whose faith in their child stands firm in the face of such raw pain, a pain that seeks to inflict collateral damage on all who dare to face it down. The winner is … nobody.

A case study on secondary trauma

I was talking to a mum we'll call Ruby the other day. We were discussing the fact that her 13-year old daughter had started ranting at her the moment she got up because of a mislaid school skirt. It was found in a pile of discarded clothes pretty soon after, but the ranting continued and every necessary activity was met with a torrent of abuse. By necessary, I mean the physical act of getting out of bed, getting dressed, cleaning her teeth and so on – mundane tasks that most 13-year olds can achieve with little effort. It was only 7.30 in the morning and the mother, Ruby, was exhausted and feeling deep despair. How was she going to pick herself up and face the day ahead? The ranting continued until her daughter was put on the school bus and the respite from the abuse was temporarily in place until 5pm struck when, after meeting her daughter from the bus, the bad behaviour continued as if the intervening hours had not occurred.

This was not an isolated event and Ruby wondered where she was going wrong. How do parents allow this level of disrespect? Why were her own moods and feelings dictated by those of her daughter? Why was she no longer in charge of her own feelings? Her emotional trauma and low mood was triggered by another person's "stuff" – not her own – so, in fact, her daughter was in charge of her mental health from the minute she started inflicting her pain on her mother.

How does secondary trauma occur?

Let me put Ruby's story in context. Ruby and her husband adopted their daughter 11 years ago. Like Eric, their daughter was severely neglected for the first two-and-a-half years of her life and has a number of issues that affect her – her ability to read the world around her and interact with others without using aggression or verbal barrages being one of them. Like us, they had to fight to get her needs recognised, the Local Authority initially saying that there was no need for a Statement for Special Educational Needs, even though the local school was unable to meet her needs on any level.

After great expense and stress, their daughter was recognised as having extremely complex needs. She needed full-time support at school and had issues with sensory understanding. The Council eventually paid for an independent school that is better equipped at meeting their daughter's needs. Even so, aggressive abuse is commonplace in their household.

This occurs in a household that was the polar-opposite of aggressive prior to their daughter's arrival: bad language was not part of their repertoire and both parents dislike and try to avoid confrontation. Their reality is now miles away from how they thought their life would evolve. This is a massive loss of aspirations and hope for them to deal with.

Coupled with this loss is the fact that Ruby held a very successful, high-powered job, but her career is effectively on hold due to the fact that getting the help her daughter so badly needs has itself turned into a full-time job. Securing a Statement and funding requires hours of letter writing, meetings and badgering of the professionals. Research is needed to evidence the fact that you need help and nobody swoops in to do this work on your behalf – it is very firmly left up to you to nag your way into receiving services and the right provision. What should be a recognised right turns into a war of attrition and the last one left standing is the one who wins, perhaps! Fighting the system is exhausting and de-skilling in the extreme, for you are fighting bureaucracy without any authority or status.

Ruby's family was too far away to be able to help and their friends were unable to cope. Ruby retrained so that her work could be more flexible, but this meant she lost a part of her life she valued greatly. She is constantly reinventing herself to find a niche in a new business arena and this has proved to be challenging and not always life-affirming as she works diligently to earn a fraction of her previous salary.

I reflected on how traumatised she sounded; how devastated and exhausted she was by the constant abuse; the feelings of wanting to run away, to heal and become whole again – but how can she when her daughter so desperately needs her?

Ruby and I had many conversations (as friends, not in a therapeutic setting) as the most important thing for her was to be heard, not dismissed. She was allowed to grieve for lost hopes, the loss of direction, the loss of her daughter. Then reconstruction began! Recognising that her child is her child – one, who despite everything, she loves dearly, Ruby began to re-emerge into her newfound professional life and gained recognition through this avenue. She accessed therapy, started meditating and knitting. Ruby began Nordic walking, which is a sociable form of outdoor exercise. Rest and recuperation were a prescription, not a luxury, and there was a need for self-acceptance and a realisation that life is hard at times. The toll her life choices have taken on her is not recognised by the outside world, nor the professionals, who are so good at constructing barriers, yet fail to see true resilience when faced with it.

The fact is that, as an adopter of a complex child, you need to fight and, at the same time, reinvent yourself, in the hope that you can carve out some sort of career and life that gives you fulfilment. Ultimately, you need to heal yourself. Is Ruby healed? Probably not fully, but is she strong enough to continue? Yes.

Secondary trauma is transmitted from one person to another, but the "receiver" is often not present at the trigger point that inflicted the harm on the individual. Neglect or abuse can be enacted upon a child throughout many of their crucial developmental stages. Current thinking is that damage can even be done in the womb, as this foetus is affected by everything the mother is exposed to, such as depression, anxiety, drugs and so on. In these early stages, the "wiring" for the unborn child is laid down. A baby born from this environment can, therefore, have a predisposition towards anxiety, affecting their ability to self-regulate, and this reduces their ability to cope with life and stress. The coping mechanisms that are developed are usually shrouded in anxiety, anger and aggression.

When a child is traumatised in their very early years (as is the case in many adoption or fostering situations), the trauma affects the child's nervous system, making the individual hyper-vigilant and suffused with adrenalin as if awaiting attack. This effect on the nervous system inhibits the child's ability to self-regulate and manage stress or anger. They push, they pull, they test love to its limits because they feel unsafe and unlovable. They try to prove this belief by destroying any relationships they have. This primary wound becomes trauma as it is unresolved and this then infects the carers because, in adoption or fostering cases, the adoptive parents' and child's nervous systems become intertwined, inextricably linked.

Secondary trauma disorder is a recognised condition, but is mainly discussed in relation to military wives. The wives (or husbands) of service personnel can suffer as a result of their partner's experiences whilst stationed in warzones. When these personnel return home, some of them bring the violence home as well. Some wives relate that they have been beaten, raped and abused at the hands of husbands suffering from Post-Traumatic Stress Disorder (PTSD).

There has also been research that recognises how some professionals, such as lawyers, teachers and the police, are also at risk of secondary trauma due to the fact that they are exposed to harrowing accounts of abuse and cruelty. They live this trauma vicariously. Adopters are largely overlooked in respect to being affected by secondary trauma – perhaps because they are unpaid? Perhaps because they do not go off sick and inconvenience an organisation? Perhaps because no one really notices?

Why are adoptive or foster parents prone to secondary trauma?

It is the very motivation and personal attributes that compel people to adopt or foster that makes them susceptible to secondary trauma. They care deeply (in most cases), are desperate to make the family work and want to maintain a loving home for their charge. As they dig in deep in order to parent the child, they whittle away at their inner reserves and their feelings of being good enough or strong enough. During this extreme dynamic of love, loss and anxiety, transference of secondary trauma occurs.

The fact that secondary trauma is affecting the family is largely ignored and this is dangerous because there is a lack of awareness about where the emotional pain originates. It is hard to understand secondary trauma unless you have witnessed living with this level of stress and anxiety for an extended period of time and so the family – particularly the primary carer and the adoptee – are judged; the parents are seen as ineffectual and "friends" do not wish their children to play with or be exposed to these "difficult" children. Help is not readily available and often the adopters are blamed for the chaos and challenges within their home environment. This judgement increases isolation and makes the carer wary of seeking help. Will they be judged again? Who will understand?

Often the fact that the relationship is not properly validated is another frustration. Adoption is undoubtedly less of a bond than birth – almost as if the adoptive parent is a childminder – so the emphasis is always on the child and what they need. The adoptive parent is almost disposable. But what is not understood or talked about is the level of abuse (often perpetrated unwittingly) that an adoptive parent suffers at the hands of their traumatised child. The behaviour exhibited is not within normal levels of tolerance and is sustained, seemingly without rhyme or reason, except from within the rationale of the traumatised child.

How to survive secondary trauma

It is important to recognise the signs of secondary trauma and act quickly. The signs can include: anxiety, panic attacks, losing one's sense of humour, being quick to get angry, headaches, tiredness, tension in the back and shoulders, a sense of claustrophobia, a loss of one's sense of self and generally not "feeling like yourself".

The routes for help can include:

- GP
- Schools (not all schools are alike and some provide greater insight than others)
- Support from adoption teams (again some post-adoption workers are fantastic)
- One's own reading and research
- Getting training
- Getting emotional support
- Getting financial help (Child Disability Allowance)
- Getting respite if you can

- Remembering your hobbies and making time for yourself
- Massage
- Counselling

Adoptive and foster parents are resilient. They survive where others would founder. Often, they say that they emerge as better people and parents and become more empathic of others. These fantastic qualities come at a cost, but most parents in this situation would not wish they had taken a different path (although there are times when they may wish they had!). Most parents would just like those agencies that set them off on this path initially to stay the course, support them correctly and grow and evolve as the adoptees do.

12

EDUCATION AND THE INSECURELY ATTACHED, TRAUMATISED CHILD

Pre-school with an insecurely attached child is often an exhausting and lonely experience for the carer. Schools do not understand the impact of poor attachment on the child, the parent, the wider family or with the child's peers. Any training there is on attachment seems to largely miss the mark and input on additional needs for teachers is limited and can be ineffective. Unfortunately, many teachers do not even know what attachment means and do not wish to have a relationship with the child, worrying that becoming the "safe adult" will be too time-consuming and emotionally draining. One SENCO even confused attachment and autism. Little or no thought is given to the parents who shoulder the burden of their child's behaviour day in and day out without respite. Teachers can choose to disengage or avoid the child, but parents cannot.

Some teachers do naturally understand such children and their needs and they work seamlessly with them on a relational level, but these are the exception rather than the rule. Those teachers who fail to understand the child in their care leave them feeling chaotic and abandoned. They then go home, clutching the hurts acquired during the day – the wounds that are inflicted because they do not fit in – and share these deeply troubled feelings with their families in the only way they know how: through the medium of anger. Sadly, the child and the family are then placed into a position of conflict with the school, the teachers and often the Local Authority. Help is needed and sought out, but often not given. Schools like to explain in detail the wrongdoings of the student, but rarely do they look to their own practices and seek different ways of being, of connecting. Accountability is not robust and pastoral teams shoulder most of the responsibility for these children that do not "fit in", but they often lack training and support.

All too frequently, the attachment disordered child is "managed" by exclusion or isolation – using the same strategies that are imposed on other students. A consequence of this behavioural management system is that the needs of the young person are overlooked. Difficult behaviour should tell the teacher that a person is unhappy, that it is a symptom of other things going on, but, sadly, behavioural management techniques look at the symptom, not the cause. All too often, a young person's education is ignored because they are repeatedly missing classes, so, consequently, these behaviours overshadow the need to learn.

Bright children with attachment disorders often emerge without any qualifications and then what will they do with their life? Children with attachment issues end up with a Special Educational Needs Statement, a label for life. Specialist help is rare and hard to come by. Often, because the parent/carer has to go to war to get additional help for their child, the adult becomes the combatant, when all they really want is help. One parent said that she had fought so hard to get her child a SEN Statement, that once it was achieved, she felt bereft. After all, who wants their child to *need* an SEN provision? But SEN and adoption are often bedmates, thus creating more obstacles for them and their parents to overcome.

The toll it takes on the carer

The parent who is the main carer of an insecurely attached child is primarily at risk of secondary trauma, but it can also affect their marriage or relationship. It is reported that 80% of marriages or relationships that are caring for a child with special education needs end in separation or divorce – the very last thing that an adoptive child needs.

The carer directly picks up on the internal turmoil that their child is feeling and transference of trauma is common. The ability for the parent to receive the signals of distress is vitally important for the connection and understanding necessary to assist in the parenting of children experiencing attachment issues. However, the carer must develop their own boundaries, so that they can remain calm, rational and resourceful.

The very demands of parenting through attachment mean that the parent cannot become too removed behind their own boundaries of self-care as this can be seen as abandonment and cause the child to further spiral and panic and so their behaviour issues can escalate. A consequence of this is that the parent/carer has limited recovery time and so the physical, mental and emotional toll is unremitting. The parent can lose a sense of themselves and their identity.

The feeling of no longer being the author of your own mood is frightening. The parent's mood is dictated by a ball of energy who may only be two-years old. "Take time out, take care of yourself, don't just focus on your child all the time", are common refrains – but babysitters are few and far between and not many people volunteer to look after a traumatised child. In addition to this, the traumatised child cannot attend after-school clubs, holiday clubs or other everyday activities that give family members time out because of their behaviour. This can put immense strain on relationships. When can parents recharge ready for the next confrontation?

13

ATTACHMENT DISORDER

Living with an attachment disordered child

Attachment disorders are challenging. The behaviours expressed can easily be mistaken for that of a person with autism, Asperger Syndrome, challenging behaviour and commonly, ADHD. In my experience, attachment disorder can express all of the above types of behaviour, but also none of them in the classical sense, so an attachment disordered child does not fully fit any one category. They can float in and out of the key characteristics in a seemingly disparate manner. In certain settings, when they are calm, you may not even consider that the person has an attachment disorder. Therefore, the test for an attachment disorder needs to be conducted in different environments to fully assess the person and provide a correct diagnosis.

The key behaviour that was expressed as part of Eric's attachment disorder was extreme temper tantrums:

uncontrollable ranting and rage. He was calm one minute, raging the next, for no apparent reason. The word "No" was often the precursor, but not always. His temper would flare over some small factor, such as which trainers to take to school, his feelings quickly escalating to slamming doors, kicking things (even dogs if they were in the way), screaming and being abusive to anyone in the family.

His face would contort, puce with anger, and yet there was a slight smile at the back of his eyes because he got enjoyment from making other people suffer. He would laugh inanely, run away from me, then taunt me, upping the ante until there was no alternative except intervention because, otherwise, harm would befall him or others. His reasons for his outbursts were often repeated endlessly, but are rarely justified, and I got a real sense of "game on" because his goal now was to annoy and eventually enrage me. And so the secondary trauma transference occurs.

Eric was selective as to whom he showed his temper. For a few months my husband did not witness it – he just heard secondhand how the day had gone, which was rarely well. The social workers did not witness it. I filmed him once to show people the level of aggression I endured because I felt that nobody fully saw or believed what I went through, day after day. I have often felt that I would never accept this type of behaviour anybody else. If Eric were my husband, we would be divorced.

As Eric grew, the anger grew with him in size and ferocity. He became less selective about sharing his bad temper. He shouted at my husband, my other children, my sister. He created a scene anywhere and everywhere. Every outing was met with, "I don't want to go there/do that." He has had to be removed from many a premises, he has missed activities and been physically carried out of shops. Each family activity is tempered by the thought, "Can I cope with Eric in this situation?"

And, woe betide us if a plan had to be changed. The fact that a café was not open once was a major trigger, leading to a massive meltdown. Needing to go to another shop that I had not previously disclosed to him created a major tantrum. This is where autism and attachment cross over. Routine is important, but more important to Eric is control. Eric needs to control all activities in the family. Everything is manipulated so that he has control: "Well, if I do that, can I do this …?" Again, this could be construed as being autistic because the behaviour presents as rigidity and an inability to bend.

As the primary carer, I am in the privileged position of being met with all his insecurities full on. He calls me names, swears at me, hits me and manipulates me. If I cry, it scares him. If my mood is not level, it makes him worse. I am the parent that must be there at all times, must always be calm, not too happy, not too sad. I cannot express grief, as this upsets his balance. I have to brush myself off, not bear grudges, be ready to accept his apology, greet him from school with love. Professionals state that I need to be ready to re-engage with him when his mood returns to a steady state, but nobody really tells you how to do this.

Since having Eric, I am no longer in charge of my own moods. I have to be "happy-ish" always. If he is in a good mood, all is well. If he wakes up in a bad mood, then soon all the family take on his mantle. He is in a very powerful position. I sometimes feel that I should ask him what I think about a certain subject as I feel that he controls my moods and my thoughts. He is all encompassing in his needs.

The ADHD part of him means that he cannot relax. He is always talking, asking incessant questions, demanding interaction from the minute he is up in the morning or sets foot inside the door. He cannot come into a room quietly, he is noisy, and questioning, announcing his presence from a distance. Each thing that he does is met with the next thing he wants to do. He cannot entertain himself. He has never played games, drawn pictures or done jigsaws. He wants all my attention, all of the time. Living with Eric is bit like living in a vacuum. Only he exists and it's like he forbids the air to enter the room – he saps energy and oxygen. Eric is exhausting. This impacts our girls as they hate seeing me hurt and they also know that they must retreat to their rooms in order that they do not get sucked into the abuse – but they can still hear the tirades as they flow. I defend them as rigorously as I fight for and with Eric. They are kind girls who are protective, but never blame him or us as parents. They accept that Eric is their brother and they love him. They have an empathy that has a depth to it that transcends their years on this earth. I still worry for them.

Eric also hates change and is adept at transmitting his insecurities onto others. The feelings he engenders are a direct reflection of the abyss he feels himself. In the face of his moods, I feel my heartbeat accelerating and my thoughts becoming confused. I feel engulfed, angry, sad, upset, even though I realise that these are feelings telegraphed from him as I become the lightning rod to his emotions. He may be unable to describe his feelings, but he is very good at drawing the adult into his chaotic world. I am not a chaotic person or should I say that I never was until I parented Eric. He has changed me, sometimes for the good, sometimes for the not so good. I am less sure of myself and my abilities, but, in other ways, I see things more clearly. I can weed out the significant from the insignificant. I can prioritise.

Living with someone with an attachment disorder is like living with a volcano, always waiting for the next eruption, for the lava to spew forth and engulf you. It is not a relaxing life. One adoptive parent I spoke to (who also lives with a child with attachment issues), said, when I asked if she was looking forward to a relaxing holiday, "No, but being at home is not relaxing either. We may as well be unrelaxed in the warm." Living with an attachment disordered child is a life without peace or respite. Holidays and weekends just mean more of the same, but magnified. Respite, even for a short while, if you can scratch out this time at all, is met with anger and the feeling that you let your child down by abandoning them. The payback is often violent and protracted, the benefit of respite wiped out the minute you re-enter their orbit.

The other facet of Eric is his empathy. He can be kind, funny, generous and loving. He likes to socialise (though he often gets this wrong with his peers); he adopts old ladies, who he genuinely likes. He is loyal, tenacious and determined. He defies definition. He is complexity itself.

Attachment Disorder Theory

The main person linked with the Attachment Theory is John Bowlby (1907-1990), who described attachment as being "an emotional bond with another individual or individuals". He was a psychoanalyst who linked mental health and behavioural issues with early childhood care and he believed that children and babies have evolved with a basic need to stay connected in order to ensure their survival. The primary attachment (normally maternal) provides a blueprint for future relationships. If this attachment is not there or is disrupted, then the child does not feel secure, affecting their long-term cognitive abilities, as well as their ability to connect in future relationships with other adults or their own children. Affected individuals can have ongoing issues with anger, anxiety and an inability to give and receive affection.

Mary Ainsworth researched this further in the 1970s and developed Bowlby's theories with the "Strange Situation" study, which observed children from 12-18 months old and how they responded to being left and then reunited with their mums. Ainsworth identified three main styles of attachment (Cherry, 2016. p.1):

1 Secure.

2 Ambivalent-insecure.

3 Avoidant-insecure.

Disorganised-insecure attachment was added on by further research by Main & Solomon in 1986 (Cherry, 2016. p.1), where the child may present as confused and avoid their parents. This has been linked with inconsistent behaviours in parents and this makes the child feel unsure about the response they will receive.

Some contributory factors to Attachment Disorder are:

- Neglect (physical and emotional).
- Abuse (physical, sexual, verbal).
- Separation from primary carer (illness, death, imprisonment, adoption, fostering).
- Inconsistency from primary carer (daycare, nannies).
- Change or frequent moves (foster homes, orphanages).
- Trauma (serious illness or incidents).
- Depression in primary caregiver.
- Addiction of primary carer.

- Lack of parenting skills and/or support (young mothers/fathers, sufferers from attachment issues themselves).

Attachment is believed to be influential on an individual's life and secure attachment leads to better self-esteem and better coping skills, meaning that they can achieve more in life, form positive relationships and suffer less from mental health issues.

The reality of living with attachment disordered young people cannot be fully understood by reading the theory alone, so I have included some quotes from individuals to try and portray the stress that this condition can exert upon families and on the children themselves.

Quotes from parents

> *"I feel as if I have woken up in the House of Commons every day. I have gone through so many arguments by 9am that I am exhausted. I spend the rest of the day recovering, readying myself for her coming home."*
>
> —Debbie

> *"My mood is dictated by my child. I have to be calm all the time and any chinks in my mood make things more difficult."*
>
> —Sue

"She says the most awful things to me, the abuse is off the scale, but I need to not react and always be there. I am knackered."

—Ann

Quote from an attachment disordered child

"I feel so angry, I want to hurt myself to stop the feelings. People don't understand me. I hate school. I hate feeling like this."

—Mike

"Everything feels unsafe."

—Anon

"I feel angry, stressed up to a level 7 (out of 10) every day when I go into school. I then get more stressed every day. I can't think then – it is too much for me."

—Eric

"I love you, but I hate you. I would be better off living somewhere else ... I love you."

—Eric

ATTACHMENT DISORDER

"My head feels 'buzzy' all the time."

—Anon

Parenting an attachment affected child

It can largely be claimed that we learned how to parent or at least learn our style of parenting from our own parents. Our routines, attitudes, ways of celebrating family events are learned from our own family. There are exceptions, as with most things, so some people who have excellent parents become neglectful parents themselves and, equally, those adversely affected by bad parenting can resolve to be the opposite and teach themselves to be kind, giving parents.

The parenting issues of an attachment disordered child are very complex because the way we want to parent our children – the way we want to be as parents – is not what our child might need. Parents of these children have to forget what they thought they knew about parenting and learn new methods. Knee-jerk responses to an attachment disordered child have to be filtered.

Normally, children adapt to the adult and modify their behaviour accordingly, learning how to avoid conflict by assessing what behaviour works and what doesn't. If a parent is annoyed, they show it and may be cross and remove privileges and eventually the child learns to adapt their behaviour (or completely rebels in their teens, but this another issue!).

A child with attachment issues, however, lacks this ability to moderate their behaviour. They are anxiety-driven, hyper-vigilant and, mainly, scared. Threats and sanctions do not seem to compute. In that heightened moment of anger, the amygdala swamps the frontal cortex of the brain with adrenal hormones, preventing reasoning from kicking in. Consequences are of no value because the attachment issue affected child cannot think beyond the here and now. They are a bag of adrenaline and they can seem to be dangerously out of control.

This feeling of being out of control can all too easily be transposed onto the adult, who then becomes stressed, lacking an anchor in a raging sea and at a loss as to how to "make" their child behave. Both parties are lost. Shouting only ramps up the conflict because the child or young person draws energy from the adult, feeding their fear. They then react as if they are plugged in to an electricity socket, laughing inappropriately and being massively defiant. This behaviour is frightening to behold.

Professionals advise the carer to remain calm and stay in control, but the reality of living with this behaviour is massively stressful. Parents cannot just walk away to a life of sanity. The reality is that this behaviour can meet you in the morning, the evening, before bed, at the weekends and will accompany you on holiday – basically, wherever I travel, my bundle of stress comes with me!

14

SEEKING HELP BUT GAINING LABELS

Seeking help and support is an uphill struggle. In my experience, asking for help is demeaning, exhausting and triggers trauma and shame. Each meeting with a "professional" requires that we go through every facet of our life to date – again. The telling of it is sad and rehashes things best left forgotten. They want the details, but they do not read the numerous files already assimilated, so, each time, we have to start the whole sorry story all over again – another two hours out of our lives, purely to get that person up to speed. But verbal repetition of the trauma creates further trauma and each of these "airings" creates another onslaught of emotion that then has to be absorbed and coped with, on top of the behaviours presented daily by Eric.

As far as I can see, everyone works in "silos" separate and distinct from each other, even when they belong to the same organisation, such as Social Services, or, indeed, work in the same room. All these individuals are extremely busy – or so they never tire of telling me – and really don't know what they can actually "add". I found contacting Post-Adoption Services in Stockport extremely taxing. At a point when you are at your lowest ebb and have accepted that you need help, the actual task of finding someone to talk to is a mission in itself. Their website has no direct links and phone calls were passed from pillar to post and then the call, more often than not, was dropped. The thought of repeating the process was often too much to bear. This is my experience with one local organisation, but I'm willing to bet that I'm not alone in this.

When eventually I did get through, I was met with a very abrupt post-adoption social worker, saying rather callously, "Well, what is it you want?" A better starting place might have been to ask what they could do to help me. The devil is in the detail. Eventually, a social worker arrived, but offered no real help. Her promise to, "Get into that school to teach them about attachment issues," was just another empty promise of action never to come.

Meetings are attended, if attended at all, by any number of such long-suffering, quick to moan individuals who offer no hope for the future. They are often off sick, so there is no continuity of process, which is incredibly frustrating. Sick leave by Speech and Language specialists (S & LT), social workers and educational psychologists is at epic proportions, but is accepted as the norm. The parents of the child do not have this luxury.

I asked for support for Eric repeatedly at primary school, Kingsway, and Castle Hill. I asked for Educational Psychology support from Year 5 onwards. He was eventually assessed in the June of Year 6 and CAMHS was recommended, but nearly two years later, still no support had been afforded to us. Many notes were taken and filed, never to be read again. We had two years of meetings with a mental health practitioner – when she was not off sick – but the meetings were at least three months apart and completely unproductive. Therapy was not an option apparently.

Eventually, we got to see an associate child psychiatrist for the first time, but only because Eric wrote about the desire to no longer be here at all as, for him, suicide seemed to be a way to get away from his pain. This was devastating to hear from such a young child, as it is from anyone, but was a clear message that he felt absolutely overwhelmed by his life and that we could not help him enough. We hoped for some great insight – up until now unseen – but were once again disappointed. Notes were not read ahead of time and, once again, we had to repeat our situation, which meant old wounds were revisited and, therefore, deepened. The associate psychiatrist spoke to Eric and believed all that he said, like that he'd not been eating or sleeping, which was untrue and I pointed this out, but this was seen as a challenge to the diagnosis of low mood. I agreed he had low mood, just not with the issue of sleep and diet. My perceived challenge was not well met!

CAMHS insisted that they could not help Eric until the ADOS (Autism Diagnostic Schedule) was completed in order to determine whether or not autism was part of the mix we were dealing with. It seemed that no help could be offered until this had been done, so we waited and waited for the test – a test that I fundamentally object to, by the way. It is a medical model and, in my experience, being labeled as autistic does not help to manage people or help them learn to manage themselves. However, apparently the system cannot be beaten, so wait we did. A diagnosis of moderate autism was now bestowed upon our child, but the help we received was non-existent! Our world was not altered in any way other than that we were summarily ejected from CAMHS after months of inactivity and apathy. The final meeting was held about Eric's autism, S & LT (Speech & Language Therapy) was recommended and then the discharge ensued. Case closed!

The other diagnosis Eric received was of ADHD (Attention Deficit Hyperactivity Disorder). I did not want Eric to take the medication for ADHD that was offered to him. It is a Class A drug and has many side effects, just like any other drug. I was concerned about medicating a child, turning him into a shadow of his former self. ADHD is a challenging condition, but is also who Eric is. I was scared of losing too much of his essence. I looked on the Internet for answers, but all the websites I came across recommended therapeutic interventions before or alongside the administration of Ritalin-type drugs.

I looked into Neurofeedback as an option, but this had not been adequately evaluated at that time, so it was not an option for us. During a Neurofeedback session, sensors are used to track brainwaves, showing the individual when their brain is being calm or agitated. The information can then help the person to learn to control their own impulses. I also looked into 'Take Ten', a computer programme designed to provide this kind of information in the shape of a game that had been developed by a guy called Fintan from Northern Ireland in response to issues presented by his son. I managed to get hold of Take Ten, but Eric refused to engage with it. Another door closed.

The only option then was to medicate Eric. I remember the Team Around the Child (TAC) meeting where I was told in the reception immediately prior that Eric had scored 90% on the ADHD test he had taken at CAMHS. The test consisted of Eric sitting in front of a computer screen and having to stay focused enough throughout the test to accurately click on images at the right time. For someone with ADHD the task is hard due to their inability to concentrate for long periods of time. 90% meant that Eric had serious issues with his ability to focus and concentrate, with the classic signs of ADHD being that the child is unable to sit and complete tasks and they are often impulsive. I had no time to assimilate the information and expressed my concerns regarding medicating a 13-year old boy. This was met with disbelief by the few people at the meeting – why would I not wish to medicate? But my online research hadn't provided any alternatives and my discussion with Derm left us feeling that we had no choice but to agree to the medication regime they were advocating. We then had to wait from June 2015 until November 2015 to see the paediatrician before the drugs could be prescribed. Although we weren't keen on him taking the drugs, once we had come to the decision, we were made to wait another six months and we felt the delay was ridiculous and just compounded the damage that was inflicted on us over those months.

The paediatrician was lovely with Eric though, taking the time to answer any questions and explain ADHD in a way that we could all understand. It is actually over-stimulation, like looking at a firework display, but seeing all of the fireworks go off at once, and being unable to focus on one because they were exploding together. Someone without ADHD can see a rocket set off, climb and then watch and admire the colourful explosion in the night sky, before refocusing on the next rocket or Catherine wheel. ADHD means that there is too much going on, all of the time.

I spoke in early July 2015 with a young man who had personal experience of an ADHD drug. He had been diagnosed as having Asperger Syndrome. He was very articulate and happy to share how it felt for him.

He said that whilst taking the drug, he felt that he was unable to access a part of himself, as if it was in effect "locked away" whilst on the medication. But in class he could totally focus on the lesson as all distractions were eliminated. He said that this was very helpful as he was easily distracted by anything and everything. He did state that he did not find it easy to form friendships though as he felt "cut off". He could get his homework done and organise himself though.

However, the amount of medication had to be reduced as the drug seemed to exacerbate his anxiety problems. Therefore, for his exams, he reduced the amount taken. He did not take it at weekends or when on holiday either as he said that the drug had helped him to learn some mechanisms for coping with these situations.

He is no longer on the drug and is in Year 11 and going to drama college. He said that he could not take the medication if he wanted to act as he needed to access his emotions in order to perform, which apparently he is amazing at! He now seems to be able to cope well without the drugs. Interestingly, his parents could not see a downside and his father, in particular, was actively promoting the medication, although his mum was a little more circumspect. She said that, before taking the drug, they sought advice from a private psychiatrist, but have not regretted their decision, feeling that their son could not have achieved what he has and would not have stood a chance of getting any qualifications without the drugs and that they gave him "amazing clarity of thinking". She said she knew when he was in a state at school before he was taking the medication, that something was wrong because they were always being called in to school and he was unable to focus at all. He had other issues too that primary school did not pick up. Sadly, she also said that he did not have one friend either in school or outside it.

She certainly did not push me into making a decision about Eric, she just advised me to go with my best instincts. Her son was thoughtful and clear about the effects of medication and I could see in him a young man who had a sense of self, a sense of direction and who was succeeding in spite of, or maybe because of, the issues he had had to overcome.

So, I could see the benefits and felt that Eric needed to be given every chance afforded to him to succeed in this life, so we agreed to start Eric on the medication, Methylphenidate, as advised. One of the side-effects of the medication can be a loss of appetite and a feeling of nausea. Eric has experienced both of these, albeit the nausea wore off after a few weeks. The loss of appetite remains, however, but he is still growing upwards and he now towers over me! Eric began to engage more at school though and, within a few months, was no longer in Isolation with such regularity. In his words, "I feel calmer and my head is clearer". At last, he was more able to think before acting.

A few months after the initial test for ADHD, he sat it again. He did two tests: one without the medication and then after having taken it. The results were amazing.

He was able to focus throughout the test and showed a "normal" response. The medication was working for him. He could concentrate more readily and engage better at school. I still feel saddened that chemicals in this day and age are the only options on offer and also that it took so long to diagnose him because the signs were all there from his early days at primary school, but, nonetheless, it is working. Another effect has been that Eric is slowly building up a small group of friends and is now seen as being a good example by some of the younger students. He is on the School Council and does sports leadership – this would not have been the case without medication.

The TAC (Team Around the Child) meetings were a farce. I asked for them to be called as I was all too aware that the services were disjointed to say the least. It was an attempt to draw everyone together and coordinate things for Eric. TAC meetings are supposed to remind everyone that the child is central to the process, but it just served to remind me that it was a misnomer! Most meetings consisted of me, Derm and the SENCO.

The first meeting held by the SENCO had me in tears for the full hour, with not one word of sympathy or even a tissue offered: cold, clinical indifference was overlaid with her feelings of righteous indignation that I, a parent, had been presumptuous enough to ask for the TAC meetings in the first place. How dare I!

The meetings stumbled on until early in 2016, when they were finally halted, but I can honestly say that the social workers, S & LT, CAHMS and the educational psychologist attached to the school, who met Eric once, all treated the meetings with equal amounts of disdain and low import. Child first? I think not! Did it draw resources together? No!

Our experience with the post-adoption social worker was no more invigorating. Because we had adopted through MAS, our support was to be provided through them, but, sadly, when they closed their doors due to lack of funding, our support died with them. We were supposed to be transferred to Stockport Post-Adoption Services, but we were not given an individual to contact. MAS closing also meant that our contact with a psychiatrist ended. I tried on several occasions to seek support, but got passed around departments as there was no direct number provided on the website. These attempts were made in times of desperation and I ended up getting on with things myself – probably not my best decision. Eventually, I did get through to the right people and a post-adoption worker was allocated to us after about six years without support. As with all these meetings, I had to repeat Eric's life story and the subsequent events and notes were duly taken. Then the judgements came, regarding our wayward 13-year old son's smoking: "Just let it go, Laura." And when I said that he needed therapy around anger, anxiety and self-esteem, she questioned, "Are you the right person to be saying this, Laura? Are you?" Her tone was patronising in the extreme. When I spoke of EMDR (Eye Movement Desensitisation and Reprocessing) as an option for therapeutic intervention, she looked blank and dismissed it. I could access it privately, but not through them. The fact that a Post-Adoption Fund existed for therapy was not talked about.

It seemed to me that the "support" part of the Post-Adoption Service was missing from her job description. The only thing on offer was that I could attend parenting courses run by her! I had attended the Webster Stratton course some years ago at the behest of our MAS social worker, Lynne, and had not enjoyed the process. The Youth Offending Service group was even worse, which we all attended in the June of 2015, as there was nothing else available. Sitting in groups with other struggling parents does not help me. I always end up trying to help them and just come away feeling overburdened.

After one particularly difficult morning, I was talking to a friend at British Military Fitness (BMF) about my day. It was the first time that I had articulated the thought properly, but I said that all I really wanted was someone I could call when things went wrong; someone who would prioritise seeing me quickly, who would sit with me, talk, listen and have empathy for my plight. I know there would not be any quick answers, but together we might find a way of coping, a strategy for going forward, having "kicked the cat", so to speak. I wanted a mentor who knew more than me, but truly understood the path I was on. I realised that nowhere in my life was I able to get this support and, in fact, it only became available to me from January 2016 after a complete meltdown and crisis in our home – but more of that later!

I have always hated labels because they limit potential in many respects. Outsiders only see the "diagnosis" – in Eric's cased ADHD – and avoid or excuse themselves from contact; the individual with the label can believe that they are sum of these parts and no more. I wanted Eric to live a "normal" life and not to be viewed as being different, but I have had to accept that this was not practical or, indeed, helpful for him.

The way society copes with differences is to categorise them, to box them off. I wanted Eric to dream and achieve all that he was able to, but the educational and health systems are not designed like this. It was through labeling him as being a certain person that gave Eric access to medication that helped him concentrate with his ADHD; the autistic label gave him some one-to-one hours in the community with Independent Options (Aiming High Breaks contracts Independent Options to provide this support) and allowed him to enter the autistic hub at his school where he was understood and really liked, for probably the first time. The label of pragmatic language impairment explained his communication issues. I know that these interventions are helping, but I believe that an open, accepting mind from professionals would have helped him more whilst we were waiting to be seen at CAMHS. Many strategies in the hub are about liking the child, understanding their behaviour and putting the necessary support in *for the child*. This approach could and should transcend the autistic hub environment. ADHD, Autism and Attachment are all anxiety driven – therefore, therapeutic approaches such as Lifespan Integration Therapy could actually be first port of call for these young minds and then further interventions could follow on as necessary. The calmer the child, the better their relationships and their self-esteem.

15

ACCEPTANCE AND HOPE

Two people recently have told me that maybe I just need to accept that Eric is the way that he is for the sake of my mental health. I question whether they would sit back and accept it if their precious child was so sad and unhappy. I think not. The striving to make things better for Eric is what keeps me relatively sane. I am a natural problem solver, a seeker of solutions. I research in the knowledge that I do not have all the answers, but someone else may well be further ahead than myself and that maybe some new research is being conducted that is not yet mainstream, but may eventually help him. That may be tilting at windmills, perhaps, but each journey starts with a single step and it gives me hope!

The USA is streets ahead of us: they have whole organisations set up around attachment and trauma; they have schools that are run on an attachment-based philosophy; they use cutting-edge therapies such as Neurofeedback, EMDR, yoga and Emotional Freedom Techniques – therapies that deal with the somatic (body) presentation of trauma and pain. In comparison, the UK is a barren wasteland of hopelessness, medication and long-term mental health issues for many unfortunate souls. So, I cannot sit back and watch Eric collapse until I have tried every avenue. Acceptance is not an option for me. I know for a fact that most of the professionals that I have encountered to date know less on the subject than I do and have less drive to learn about it too. When I broach the research that I have done, I am met with blank stares and the patronising response that the fact is not recognised within the NHS or Social Services.

For example, the Associate Psychiatrist we met with had heard of Pathological Demand Avoidance (PDA), but as it was not recognised in the Pennine Trust, so she could not diagnose it. I brought it up as a possibility because I'd happened to see a documentary on it and other Trusts were recognising it as a diagnosis within the autistic spectrum. The documentary showed a boy of around eight years of age who had a complete meltdown when asked to perform the simplest of tasks such as brushing his teeth. This behaviour was so similar to Eric's and was "anxiety-based" and I felt this diagnosis had to be at least eliminated – but my suggestion was completely ignored.

I have learnt that most of the "professionals" I have encountered are threatened by new scientific advances and an enquiring mind such as mine. They are happier providing a "cookie cutter" approach to most cases and thinking outside the box is frowned upon. I think that because I question and research, I threaten their authority and, therefore they try and close me down. Each shut down is a further cut to my already scarred skin.

I would love to hand over our lives, our case, to a safe pair of hands, a pair of hands that has our son's and our family's best interests at heart; someone who would advocate on his behalf without thinking about budgets and time – I would happily accept their advice. But, in my experience, we are his best advocates and case managers. No one else is really that interested or that motivated. It's sad, but true.

Hope, however, comes in strange guises. School had closed for the Easter holidays, Eric being in Year 8 in 2015, but he was not in a good place and was threatening suicide. Needless to say, the girls were distraught and I myself was emotionally worn down and becoming ill. Dermot felt sad for me and for Eric, but was also struggling in a job that was making him feel stressed. He says himself that his way of coping was to mentally remove himself. The specialist school were ringing us saying that they were running out of options for Eric and, after the half-term, we would have to look at other options. What they were, I had no idea. I did know that I felt that school was killing him. He was scared, anxious and had lost all sense of who he was. It seemed he was trying on different personas like a model at a clothes show. "If I look like a hard man, they will leave me be. If I shave my head, I will look tough. If I pretend to smoke I will fit in …" This was in the period after the ADHD diagnosis, but during the six-month wait to see the paediatrician who would prescribe medication for him. Eric's attitude, walk, language – it was offensive on so many levels. I was losing my boy. He was losing himself.

For the Easter break, Eric went to Belfast with his dad, so that I could give some time and space to the girls, one of whom was in the middle of her GCSEs and finding his behaviour really hard to tolerate. When he returned from his holiday, Eric was great – relaxed, calm, talkative, non-combative, funny and polite! And, after being home with us for several days, the lovely boy remained. This display of good behaviour renewed my hope. Inside him, *is* a good boy who just needs help to manage his anxiety and relationships. Behavioural interventions miss the point for Eric. He needs to feel safe and valued and in a calm environment. Then he can join in, contribute and learn. So, there is always hope and I cannot just accept his fate.

Sometimes, though, it is hard to hold on to hope when parenting a child like mine. To most parents, our daily life with all its stresses and strains would be unimaginable. I was speaking to high school teacher whist at British Military Fit and we were discussing Eric. She began offering advice and I assume she was trying to be helpful, but it was so simplistic, it was verging on patronising: "You have to demand this … You need to do that ... Have you tried ..." Yes, we have tried all of the above, and, yes, we have pushed for more support, in fact – you name it, we've tried it.

We have run headlong into so many walls that it feels like we are in an endless loop, mere characters within a video game with an invisible master controller managing our movements and erecting barriers that only they see – until we run into them. We have no map, no means of navigation, no lights, no idea where to head or where we will end up. It's like we are the entertainment. Onlookers heckle, judge, sit back and smugly analyse our dilemmas. They try and make us feel better by reminding of Eric's good qualities, but this gets so tiring. Sometimes it just feels too much and I lose hope – but who I can say that to?

I have never been a jealous person, nor do I wish for others to struggle through life like I do – but sometimes the calm family units that surround me, the successful, uncomplicated children flourishing in private schools, facing complex career choices (shall I be a doctor or a dentist? Oxbridge or Bristol?) is too much to bear. I am that parent that puts others' woes into perspective: "God, and I thought *I* was having problems ..." I can play the game of one-upmanship to a tee, as, whatever drama you encounter, I have a bigger, better T-shirt with loads of profanity to accompany it.

During each stage of this journey of loving Eric, I feel that I am in a lift shaft and the cable is fraying. The lift lurches out of control, then jars to a sudden violent stop. The doors open and I stick my head out, becoming slowly orientated to the new reality, only for the doors to slam shut, narrowly missing my head, taking me down to a new, lower level, a new reality. This level then becomes the new normal. Then, unbeknownst to me, the cable frays again and we plummet and adjust as life goes on. I keep thinking that I have reached the bottom, but apparently not. It is hard to hold on to hope in this situation.

16

THE CRISIS

After 11 years of asking for help, the unimaginable happened. Eric made an allegation in early October 2015 – a false allegation against his dad – to a teacher at school. Eric claimed that his dad had hit him. I was there at the time Eric alleged the abuse and it did not happen, but my view was never sought.

The night before the allegation, the evening followed a predictable path. Eric was angry – raging, in fact, but over what, I do not know. He was picking holes in me from the minute he came home from school up until the time he went to bed. He kept on upping the ante, striving for interaction and conflict. He was smirking and gibing at us all in equal measure, going from one to the other. The girls made a rapid exit from the dinner table and hid in their rooms, knowing that he was in one of his uncontrollable moods. The dogs retreated to the utility room, also knowing that they would be threatened or kicked at – just his volume made my gentle dogs quake.

I could not retreat. Instead, I tried to not interact or react to his rudeness. I started to work on the computer that was set up in the open-plan kitchen area. Eric was patrolling behind me, getting more wound up, in spite of me trying to bring him down. He started throwing things around and I felt that he might well hit me from behind because he was intimidating and unpredictable when in this kind of mood. He tried to throw the computer off the table.

On numerous occasions, he was asked to go to another room or his bedroom in order to calm down. I told him to take some time away from me as I was the catalyst for his anger, but he refused. He continued to stoke his fury by taking runs past me, making digs, seeking to wound me. There was no sign of his temper calming down and eventually Derm told him to go to bed. Eric refused to leave the room, threatening both of us physically. Derm tried to remove him from the kitchen, but Eric, as he always did, deliberately fell to the floor, laughing. Eventually, he did leave and go to his room after much profanity and threats being screamed at anyone within earshot. He went to bed and eventually to sleep.

I was left feeling vulnerable and abused. I felt that even though this time he had not physically attacked me, it was coming, because his level of aggression was on the increase. Derm felt angry with his appalling behaviour and extremely unhappy with the way Eric treated me. I have always been Dermot's Achilles Heel – he is a very easygoing man, but he hates to see me upset or abused by Eric. However, this particular night was not exceptional. This sadly was the norm – this was how we lived. Therefore, I did not view the incident as being any more significant than the many that had preceded it. Before he went to school the next morning, I did try and speak to Eric, but all he would say was that Dad should apologise to him! Well, Dad was in bed and would not have apologised anyway – what for? Eric obviously went into school bearing a grudge.

Derm had retired after 30 years in the police force in May and Eric was having to adjust to both of us being around. The reality facing him was that he could no longer bully me and the girls because Derm and I could now divide and rule, by which I mean that if Eric did not wish to join in with a family outing or anything else we'd planned, then Derm would stay behind with him and I would go out with the girls and have a bit of freedom. When Derm gave his retirement speech, he acknowledged that I'd had to give up a lot to look after the children, but now he would be around to help out, allowing me time to create a life for myself. But Eric didn't like this change of circumstances and he certainly missed being able to rule the roost. His power base was eroding and he hated this – not that I was ever an easy target, but I was a lone voice, met with tirades on a daily, even hourly basis. Any leverage I'd developed to manage

Eric's behaviour just got deflected from the armour he erected around himself, rendering me powerless. I really needed Dermot's help.

In retrospect, I wonder if Eric made the allegation against his dad because he wanted "out" from the new dynamic at home where he could no longer bully me and the girls. He was well aware of the issues created by making such allegations as he had watched and learnt from his peers, some of whom had more experience of the care system. Eric had often talked about going into care, like some of his school peers. His vision of a care home was that he would end up in a Tracy Beaker type environment where the atmosphere is homely and loving and all the kids look after each other. The reality that I had witnessed whilst in the police force was a very different environment to that, where young people were vulnerable to all sorts of abuse and were corralled, not managed, and certainly not loved. Eric would have lasted less than a minute before becoming the newest victim.

Unfortunately, Eric's allegation was made to a new and inexperienced safeguarding officer and, of course, the whole safeguarding behemoth cranked into motion and, once the wheels were set in inexorable motion, they began to mow a swathe through our fragile family unit. Social Services were informed and unluckily a certain Dave* was on duty (NB: * denotes name change). He attended the school and spoke to Eric, who claimed that he had been assaulted by his father. Derm spoke on the phone to Dave openly and honestly about the argument and what had occurred. Naïvely, I feel, he trusted that the social worker would see the incident for what it was and not overreact. Derm thought it would all be okay, but I felt sick with worry. I did not believe in the impartiality of the system and, sadly, I was correct.

The next thing we heard was that Eric was refusing to come home from school and they would be looking into a temporary placement for him. I was devastated and Derm was shocked. By 5pm, Dave announced that they would bring Eric home. He and Tim* arrived at our door and assumed the position of advocates for Eric. I could tell immediately they walked in that all was not well. Dave related a "lovely" conversation he'd had with Eric about football and I could tell Dave believed that he had managed to create a deep connection with Eric – as no one else before him had ever managed to do! He had been taken in by Eric hook line and sinker – and we had been painted as the villains.

On my request, Dave discussed the issues with Eric there. This was not about shame, as the recounting of events was critical of Dermot, not Eric. This was about exploring the implications and consequences of his allegations because he had acted impulsively, out of anger. However, neither social worker wanted the stark truth told to Eric and said that such allegations would not end up with him being taken into care – they were trying to sugarcoat the reality of the situation. But, in fact, if a child is at risk, then, of course, they should be taken from the home that presents the danger. Either Eric was a victim of assault or he wasn't. I think every person making an allegation of this nature needs to understand the consequences of their actions and Eric needed to understand what he was saying.

The social workers were extremely judgemental throughout and critical when I tried to explain Eric's behaviour prior to the allegation. Apparently, the worst offence was when I said that I just wanted Eric to be "nice" – apparently, this was a totally unacceptable phrase to use. Obviously, I had missed the latest politically correct course because I did not know this was offensive!

The social workers entered our lives with pre-formed judgements and were taken in by beguiling Eric. They were so steeped in their belief that they alone could bond with this child that they ignored and failed to fully explore the true story. The lack of humanity in these so-called professionals was devastating. They judged us, ripped us apart and then left us to parent the "cuckoo" in our midst.

This process sets parents against children. No thought is given to how to heal or repair the damage created. They swanned off to their orderly lives, leaving us with a fractured family, having to rebuild in their wake. In our case, I was left with Eric and the devastated girls who bore witness to this all. The social workers did not check that they were okay or whether they witnessed anything. They were incensed, saying, "Daddy did not do that, it was Eric!", but nobody listened to them.

Derm was going home to Belfast, a pre-arranged visit, to see his mum who is in a nursing home. I have never seen someone so shellshocked and rocked to their very roots of their being as Dermot was at that time. He felt so betrayed by Eric and this was compounded by the fact that he had just retired from the police and felt such shame at this allegation being made against him. He had survived 30 years of service without receiving any complaints and now he was facing public scrutiny and the possibility of criminal charges because of an allegation from his own son.

I thought he should definitely still go to Belfast, to try and get some space for himself, but, equally, I was left trying to hold the family together. Social Services waltzed off, their only advice to us being, "Just don't be on your own with him, to prevent further allegations." I rang my sister, Elaine, in tears, and asked her to come to stay with me for the weekend. She dropped everything and came. Mum would have been so proud. My friend, Clare, invited us around for a meal to help us out, but the weekend felt surreal. It was like being left in our own private hell, unable to contact anyone or find out what was happening. Were the police going to arrive on our doorstep? Was I going to have to give a formal interview at the police station? My other feeling was one of disbelief: they came into our lives with a wrecking ball, smashed us up and then left. If Eric was really at risk, wouldn't this be a devastating scenario for a most vulnerable child?

I truly believe that any allegation of this sort would wound a family, but, with compassion and insight, the process could be far less devastating than the one we were engulfed in. Sadly, we were now escalated to Tier 3, where the help we had so desperately been asking for should be provided to us. In the many useless TAC meetings we attended, we were repeatedly told that we were only Tier 2 and, therefore, did not qualify for any help, even though we were saying that we were on our knees and the placement was threatened because of the abuse we received. Tier 2 means get on with it yourself as there is nothing we can do for you. Tier 3 is where the crisis has hit. Now, people attend meetings where previously they were too busy to care. Emergency respite for four hours could now be provided for Eric as a temporary solution for as long as Tier 3 was in force. Money is magically found to fund this from pots that were previously deemed to be empty. There was money to take him to a water park, to the gym, to go karting in Warrington, anywhere the young boys (normally) wanted to go. The man who provided this emergency respite support until the following January was an ex-teacher who carried his own wounds from flying too close to the Social Services' sun. He had been burnt by their processes too and I think we provided some therapeutic listening for him! This respite did help us temporarily, but, as soon as the crisis was deemed to have passed, the support was whipped away as suddenly as it was provided and that just meant that another person Eric connected with was removed without thought to the impact this would have on such a vulnerable boy.

The downside of Tier 3 was that the entire focus was now on our failings, not on their failure to have supported Eric adequately over the years. I suppose it felt worse because no accountability on their part existed for how appalling their service delivery had been; how many times they had let us and Eric down and left us hanging. They were pure in their eyes and we were sullied. This, for me added insult to injury.

We asked for details of the police officer who was dealing with our case, so we could contact them ourselves and arrange to go to the station to get the process started. We were told that the incident had been reported, but not to the police station where Derm had worked and no further information was offered. Nobody contacted us to see how we were all getting on either.

Our next interaction with the social worker, Tim, was at the TAC meeting on the following Thursday. It was appalling. We were in the meeting room, feeling humiliated and embarrassed with this an occupational therapist and an S & LT who we did not know and who had never attended any other meetings. Mr. Ruddick for the Hub was there, as was the school safeguarding officer who was the chair. The psychologist who had been assessing us for therapeutic input, but had not had her report verified, was also there. The first she knew of the allegation was when I informed her of recent events in the car park, prior to the meeting. Part way through the meeting, Tim decided to seize control, as there had obviously been no consultation beforehand as to how it would be managed or by whom.

I asked that the allegation should not be discussed in front of the OT and S & LT, as I did not know them. Tim

THE CRISIS

tried to force this issue, saying that he could authorise anyone to attend the meeting whom he thought should be there and that I had no rights in this area. I insisted that they had nothing to add to this discussion as they had no knowledge of the allegation or events at home. They gave their reports and left – thankfully.

Tim then decided to lambast me for my behaviour when they were at our house. He informed us that his boss had told him there would be no criminal charges or police intervention, but that his boss insisted that I be admonished about my "behaviour" when they brought Eric home. I asked him to stop as the way he was speaking to me was rude, aggressive and inappropriate. He actually held the palm of his hand up toward me to signal for me to shut up. I had never been treated like this before, but he would not be stopped. I was criticised for saying that I wanted Eric to be "nice" – I should not have said this apparently – and for the fact that I was angry with the two of them from the minute they came into my house. To be dressed down in a meeting was humiliating in the extreme. I was devastated. Mr. Ruddick did actually intervene and say that it was important we knew how much Eric loved us. This was the only kindness we received during this meeting.

The TAC meeting achieved nothing in itself, other than inflicting more wounds. The only positive seemed to be the fact that police action was not being sought. An appointment was made for Dave to come to our house on the Friday after to complete the assessment on us in accordance with Tier 3. I did not want him in the house, but resolved that we had to just get the paperwork completed and move on.

Dave was late to the arranged meeting, but the post-adoption worker was on time. Then, when Dave eventually arrived, he announced that the police had, in fact, been informed and an investigation would occur. This devastating news was delivered in an off the cuff manner, yet all he was interested in was getting the assessment done. I asked for clarification and the reasons why the decision to inform the police had been changed, but all he said was that he did not know the details. I could not understand how someone could come to deliver such devastating news without first finding out the full details. I did not see how he could, in all conscience, assess our family with neutrality as he so clearly had another agenda and our best interests were not on it!

Dave informed me that the assessment would take about 60 days to progress. I asked him to just get it over with, but he said that it would be extremely protracted and would involve many visits and interviews with our families, friends and our girls. He looked to be enjoying the news he was delivering. The post-adoption worker looked equally surprised by the turn of events – indeed, she seemed to be ambushed by this news as well. She said that we did need to know the information regarding the decision and suggested that we leave the meeting for that evening as there was little point continuing, given the circumstances. And so they left. Obviously, we were in pieces. As before, this bombshell had been given on a Friday evening and social workers all went home by early Friday afternoon, meaning we were left to stew all weekend – whilst still parenting Eric. I did complain to Dave's manager about the events and how we were feeling, mainly because I could see how devastated Derm was. I wanted our family to be protected.

Eric was getting more and more distressed, believing that all the upset should now be in the past. He had no idea of the beast he had unleashed. He was angry and wanted his Dad to be told off for getting him to leave the kitchen that night, but he did not want anything else to happen. Really, he was an innocent caught in a machine which was supposedly being driven with his best interests at heart. Yet here he was, anxious and upset and left hanging by the professionals. The only one who understood his anxiety or was willing to discuss it with him was me.

Eric did go into school and said he wanted it all to stop and that he was just angry with his dad. Social Services did talk to him and he said this to them too. In the meantime, we had been in to school to meet with the Head, who felt that the "pause" button should have been hit long before all of this happened, and that Eric was not at risk.

Life in the aftermath of the incident

The help that one would imagine should be there to help people in our situation, on Tier 3, was non-existent. We had four hours respite a week through "Short Breaks" (via social services), but that was all. We were left parenting a child who was constantly claiming he would report us every time he was told "No" – every time we set boundaries. A few weeks after the allegation, in the October half-term 2015, my lovely sister held the fort so that Derm and I could go to Malta for four nights. Elaine and I were supposed to be going together, but she felt that we were on our knees and needed the break. Elaine had never seen Derm so affected by anything. He was traumatised and had a raging migraine for the whole time we were away. On the first day of our mini-break, our middle daughter was admitted into A & E due to terrible stomach cramps. They did not know if it was appendicitis or gynaecological. I received the text but was then left with the dilemma: should we return home? As it happened, the illness was soon diagnosed as gynaecological and she was discharged with pain medication and she assured us she was okay. We never go away without the children – ever – and when we do, an emergency occurs! Did I feel the benefit of the mini-break? Yes, to a degree, but we were also mindful of returning to Eric and Social Services and the continuing fight to clear Derm's name. So it was always on our minds.

On the Tuesday after we returned home, I had a phone call from Dave, the social worker, who wanted to come and continue his assessment. I was incredulous and asked whether he was aware that I had complained about him? No, was his response. Apparently, he thought that the meeting had gone well! It was as if we had been in two different meetings or, indeed, universes. I told him that he was completely lacking in humanity and empathy and that I wanted someone else to work with – someone with an open mind and more than one "lens". He asked whether was I refusing to have the assessment done and I replied that, to be clear, I was refusing to work with *him*, not the process. He also enquired how my daughter had got on at hospital on Friday. This hit me like a grenade. The only way he could have known this personal information about my daughter would have been if the hospital or GP had informed Social Services. They would only have done this if she was considered to be at risk. The nightmare just kept getting worse. When I asked how he came by this information, he did not answer.

On returning from the break, we were faced with trying to get the complaint resolved, for all our sakes. Twice, I asked for the details about who and where the incident had been reported, but I was informed that they could not disclose that information as it was confidential! By this time, we had contacted the police ourselves and found out who was the officer involved and they spoke to Derm and visited the school to see Eric that afternoon. The matter was fully investigated and Dermot was exonerated. I believe that if we had not taken the initiative, then the case would have been left hanging in air for quite some time because there was no urgency. Eric was so relieved, he immediately calmed down at school and at home, but the girls were left feeling terrified that their dad was still going to be locked up and nobody in authority took the time to allay their fears.

Eric was given four hours of temporary extra support at weekends, but even this was of questionable value because it was deemed helpful for him to mix with other young men who were themselves struggling in one way or another, but some of them were already operating in the criminal arena and were even wearing tags! I was not at all sure that Eric would benefit positively from this experience. Other than that, there was no change: no therapeutic input and no medication, as, at this point, the paediatrician who could prescribe the medication for Eric had not seen him due to her long waiting list. It felt as if Social Services came in, ripped out our hearts and then left us to pick up the pieces.

What did I want?

- More support for Eric in an ongoing manner.
- EMDR for me and him.
- Psychological help for him.
- Getting rid of Social Services.
- Apologies for incompetence.
- Kindness.

I know that there will never be an apology from Social Services for the way they treated us after the allegation – that is, as if we were criminals. The appalling people skills of the professionals will go unaddressed and no learning will occur. My complaints have been whitewashed, with their interpretation of their effectiveness given as hard evidence. My explanation of the events and the context of our family history was ignored. The effects on us as a family were glossed over, with the people involved playing lip service only to the care of a complex child. They excuse inaction by claiming that they are working in a multi-disciplinary manner and that the inaction is in Eric's best interests. The fact that Eric received no support since he said wanted to commit suicide in March 2015 until the allegation in November 2015 was overlooked. Eric's cry for help backfired on the whole family.

17

DIARY OF EVENTS FOLLOWING THE ALLEGATION

I am including my diary entries from this period in time to give you an idea of the bureaucracy, lack of professionalism and disappointments that we faced on a daily basis. These are reproduced here pretty much verbatim – in the raw – a "snapshot" of the reality of parenting a child like Eric.

Diary: 10/11/15

Another awful TAC meeting for Eric. It is a multi-disciplinary meeting, but where are CAMHS and Post-Adoption? Where are the apologies? Surely it is only professional to tender your apologies if not attending? The dates are given at least four weeks in advance.

DIARY OF EVENTS FOLLOWING THE ALLEGATION

We arrived at 9.15am only to see Dave, the social worker we had asked not to see, in the foyer! A great start and an indicator of the meeting to come. I had asked for him to be no longer involved with our family as I felt that he had an axe to grind. When I said how I felt about his behaviour, he seemed to smirk. The manager present clearly was not impartial. The meeting progressed nothing at all. Another waste of time laced with judgement.

Three social workers, one from the "Short Breaks Service", put us on notice that their contribution is only for eight weeks, even though I know that one young man has been being supported for two years! Anyway, this is okay as they keep trying to combine Eric with other young men who are "tagged" in the judicial meaning of the word. Not great for Eric, I think.

The meeting started and, for the first 20 minutes, we discussed Eric being happier in the autistic Hub, a small unit with high staffing levels for people with an autistic label. This is true, but the next hour-plus was devoted to Social Services saying how they needed to progress their form within the time scale. They kept on saying we were unwilling to take part, but we stated clearly on many occasions that we were *unhappy with the process*, but if it had to continue, even though the original started pistol (the allegation) was unfounded, then we would co-operate, but not with Dave.

Lengthy discussions ensued, with me having to reiterate again that Dave was completely lacking in empathy, warmth and human kindness. Then we had to explain it again and again. His response was, "Well, it doesn't bother me – that's my job." He was completely lacking in any ownership of how he had come across, with no empathy (again!) or reflection of what he could have done differently. A lost cause. We said we wanted an empathic person doing the report. The lead social worker at the meeting, whose name I cannot remember, then said, helpfully, that Dave was empathic and very good at his job! I said that this was her impression as a colleague and that my experience was very different. Again, our experience was dismissed as being invalid and incorrect.

We were not told why or by whom the decision not inform the police was overturned. We were not given the minutes of the meetings as requested. The managers hide behind their desks. They could own the problem, listen to our concerns and try and resolve their poor practice. They could listen without judgement, hear and alter things positively. We do not want a pound of flesh. We are not after money. We want Eric to receive the help he needs without unnecessary delays. Sometimes people just want the chance to be listened to, for their opinion to be taken into account.

I had been contacting Social Services to voice my concerns, but still no manager would speak to me directly. We sought out legal (very expensive) advice from an expert in Special Educational Needs law. He reviewed our case and felt that the Council were not meeting the requirements set down in law with regard to Eric and his education. He advised that we take it

DIARY OF EVENTS FOLLOWING THE ALLEGATION

to court and force better provision. This was daunting and expensive – too expensive. He advised that Eric be sent into a residential school. This missed the point, in my view, about his emotional needs. Yes education is vital but, if emotionally he is lost, then a few GCSEs would not redress this fault running through his psyche. I believed and still do that we are Eric's best chance at a life that could be fulfilling.

The solicitor wrote a letter on our behalf to the Council, requesting that Dave be replaced with another neutral social worker. This did happen and a professional, obviously experienced, social worker visited us to complete the necessary form when Tier 3 has been initiated. She came and listened and met with the girls with me in the room to support them and quickly assessed the situation. She stated that she was satisfied that Eric was not at risk and that she would recommend that we were removed from this level of intervention. The Tier 3 would stay in place until Eric had his last outing at the weekend with "Short Breaks" (Social Services' emergency provision), so that the relationship that had developed could come to an agreed end. She attended the next TAC, which was run in a completely different manner from the two prior public floggings that we had been made to endure. This time it was professional, but they did not victimise us. We were deemed to be innocent. The matter was resolved in one meeting, not the months that Dave claimed it would all take.

Via the Post-Adoption Service, we had been asking for psychological support for Eric months before the allegation. The psychological report was eventually forwarded to myself after eight weeks of sitting with the post-adoption worker and her manager. The reason for the delay is unclear. The report was completed by a psychologist of their choosing, who met with us and looked at the issues presented by Eric. She completed the report which was not controversial, but was actually quite lacking in depth. It recommended six sessions around dealing with anxiety, anger and self-esteem – areas that I identified 10 months ago. The psychologist would then identify any other interventions, if applicable. Therefore, it was relatively inexpensive for the providers. A full assessment at Family Futures or the Post-Adoption Centre would have cost anywhere from £3000 to £7000 – and that is just an assessment, not interventions! This option seemed to be reasonable. The concerns were that Eric was not receiving vital input, but also that the psychologist was due to go on maternity leave and, if the therapy did not start promptly, she would not be able to work with him.

It was claimed that the delay was due to the need to work thoughtfully and in collaboration with CAMHS; that the psychological input should not counteract with the interventions CAMHS were recommending. If CAMHS had actually been working with Eric in the two years of infrequent meetings, peppered with note-taking and nothing else, then I could have understood the delay, but they had done nothing with or for him, other than assess him for autism and ADHD. We were waiting to see the paediatrician for a drugs review, i.e. Ritalin-type medication. This referral has taken nearly five months alone! Interventions recommended or tried by CAMHS: nil. What psychological input could possibly affect what CAMHS was not doing?

Medication appears to be the only option, but should be given alongside therapeutic interventions – not as stand-alone treatment for ADHD. Even in the light of the recent events, this appointment has not been accelerated. It has stood firm and will change for no man.

Diary: 11/11/15

Today we are due to see our post-adoption social worker and her manager, Faye, at the Town Hall. Faye made it clear that she'd had to alter a meeting for us! I am expecting more of the same excuses and self-righteous justification: the delays are perfectly reasonable, they are perfectly competent and are only working in Eric's best interests and so on (the implication being that we are not). The professionals are right, we the parents are wrong, again!

Really not looking forward to the meeting. Each time I feel unheard, disempowered and frustrated. I fear that I will once again fail the personality test. They will read any opposition as being an indication of my bad behaviour. It will add to the impression that I am strident and a difficult parent. This then helps them to hide from reflective practice. They are right, I am wrong. No change needs to occur. This arrogance leads to leaden organisations that fail in their service provision. It remains non-responsive. It cannot look at itself in an unemotional, non-protectionist way. It cannot tolerate that it may be flawed. Therefore, it cannot be changed.

As I said, I was not looking forward to the meeting, but Faye listened. The reasons for the eight-week delay on the psychological report and, therefore, input for Eric were not satisfactory. The delays were attributed to the psychologist needing to put more information/analysis of Eric in the report and a query as to why the report reflected changes after the TAC meeting. The change being that EMDR was suggested. I was happy with the EMDR addition – at last some therapeutic input! But it caused delay in Social Services agreeing to the psychologist's input actually occurring. They were not happy with the addition, but I was.

The psychologist had said that Social Services wanted her to amend her report. This could all have been cleared up over the phone/Skype. The delay was attributed to being unable to diarise a meeting to discuss the issues. The excuses of working with multi-agency and CAMHS was again given as "smoke and mirrors". The end result is that therapeutic input is again delayed while an appropriate therapist is identified! They did know that Dr. Pilkington would not be able to work with Eric due to her now impending maternity leave.

DIARY OF EVENTS FOLLOWING THE ALLEGATION

Leaving the meeting, Dermot and I felt better, but only because someone had afforded us the opportunity to speak about our frustrations. The recommendation for EMDR was not being actioned, as per the report, so it feels like the landscape is unchanged! It seems Social Services are resistant to using EMDR, but I don't know why. Perhaps this reluctance eventually led us to the better path of Lifespan Integration?

Diary: 12/11/15

I was informed that the social worker had been changed! I feel relief as I really did not trust him to be non-judgemental about our family. His complete lack of empathy is worrying in his role. I really felt that he was intent on destroying our fragile family, the reason being that I had failed the attitude test. I think he saw me as a "know it all", a middle-class mother who needed to be put back in her box, and that he was just the person to do it. I still do not know if he felt smug, but certainly his face took on that demeanour.

My fear is that he will never learn how much damage he wrought upon us and, therefore, other families may be met with similar lack of empathy and professionalism.

Diary: 16/11/15

We received a letter about our complaint from the service manager. Basically, the procedural error was admitted, although surrounded with excuses. The matter should have been reported to the police in the first instance, but no apologies were tendered. The way we were dealt with was dismissed as us not wanting to hear what they had to say – that we needed to hear their truth, but were not open to it. This letter, once again, totally dismissed the impact they had on our family. No offer to meet was forthcoming from the service manager. I found the letter upsetting and it reawakened feelings of frustration. The ball of anger under my left breast reformed and pulsated.

I do feel that Social Services and indeed Health and Education fail to hear what our complaint is actually saying. They investigate themselves; they feel loyalty to themselves; they protect themselves – and the parents are wrong, always! This is a particularly patriarchal approach that does not allow room to reflect or act as a reflexive practitioner. This means that learning does not take place and evolution is stunted. Surely they must allow for the fact that their impact has been damaging? Surely they should reflect and be held to account – to be honest? The expectation is that we as parents must take any criticism on any personal issue. Most parents would take great offence if their parenting style were criticised and yet they sit in judgement of parents and give their opinions freely, without censoring them, expecting the recipient to smile, accept and alter their behaviour accordingly.

I am taking it to Stage 2 of the complaints procedure, for all the good it will do! The letter said that the manager had spent time talking to the social workers involved, but the manager had not afforded us the same time or, indeed, courtesy. Hence, they were correct and professional and we were had to hear an unpalatable truth. The true version of events was never fully investigated, so conclusions were drawn without possessing the full facts or bothering to investigate fully.

Today, we were seeing the paediatrician about the prescription of Ritalin. We have been waiting for this appointment for months. The reason given is that as Eric is adopted and we do not have a full medical history, then a doctor will need to see him. We expected an in-depth investigation that warranted the delay. In fact, it consisted of a stethoscope on the chest and a blood pressure sleeve! Surely this is a complete waste of the doctor's time? The cost incurred is frightening! The delay even more inexplicable.

The doctor was very professional and allowed us to explore our concerns about the medication without prejudice. Empathy was evident, unlike when we had a similar conversation with the Associate Psychiatrist at CAMHS. We came away feeling that medication could possibly help. Hope is a dangerous thing in our experience with Eric!

Upon reading the lengthy list of side-effects for the drug, I read that this medication should not be prescribed until behavioural approaches have been tried! I have been saying that and seeking this intervention for years… This is one area that I do not really want to be proven right in.

Postscript: The last week at school, after Eric started taking the medication, has been reported as his calmest yet. I do not want to raise my hopes too high only to have them dashed.

Diary: 20/11/15

The Social Work Assessment is to be started today. The newly appointed social worker came to the house at 3.30pm. I'm not looking forward to it, but she had said on the phone that it would just be an introductory meeting and then she would arrange to return to do the assessment at a later date. The meeting was arranged for her and the post-adoption worker to do the assessment together. 3:30pm came and went – the assessor was present, but the post-adoption worker did not appear. We talked amongst ourselves. The assessor gave us a copy of the assessment form, the one that Dave claimed did not exist!

As time went on, she decided to get on with the assessment, making it clear that she saw this as a one and only visit because the child protection issue had been investigated by the police and there was no case to answer. Eric was not at risk. We discussed what had gone wrong that night. My belief is that things were becoming more structured at school with him being in the "hub". He wanted to get rid of his aggression, but the home situation had shifted as well, as Dermot was now retired. Normally, he would check out what shift his dad was on and then the challenging behaviour would start. Dermot being on night shifts or afternoon shifts were ripe opportunities for Eric to become aggressive with me. Now, with Dermot at home, Eric could no longer reign over us with his aggression. Eric wanted Dermot to be told off for making him leave the room in order that he calm down. He had no idea of the havoc he was wreaking.

The assessor did not see her role continuing. She stated that she did not really have any influence on whether or not we could access more support or, indeed, if the Aiming High Breaks/ Independent Options (four hours of one-to-one support in the community) could continue as this was under review due to funding issues. Evidently, the assessment is not about extra support, but purely to investigate the allegation. At least she was honest and above board! The assessor then asked to see the girls, but was not involved in a power play over her seeing them alone. They were reluctant to come into the room, but did co-operate and gave a flavour of themselves and our home life. During the discussion we had highlighted the lack of continuity and care. The failure of professionals to attend TAC meetings, give apologies prior to meetings and generally not having Eric at the centre of their practice. The post-adoption worker never did turn up for the meeting! No emails or texts with apologies were offered. This is not good practice and highlights the response we all too often experience. In fact, she could not have added any more credence to our concerns if she had tried!

The process is still frustrating. The importance put on this assessment by Social Services is purely because it is measurable. The child is not at the eye of the policy, nor is the family. It is all about statistics, covering their backs, and their right to be in a well-paid job, but not expected to do it with any great professionalism. The good news is that the report seems to be done. The sword of Damocles has been removed, probably to hover over some other family. Anything changed? No! Additional support? No! Protection from future allegations? NO.

The world that is Social Services continues to revolve in inept, dysfunctional circles. We are left not wanting them in our life at all. We have coped so far and will do so again. Involving them just adds to our stress. It just leads to increased expectations and then to disappointment. There seems to be no professional left, no resources, no willingness to help. When there is blame to be lashed around, they are your people – just do not expect empathy, competence or care. Saying that, I liked the assessor. She was professional, human and kind with the children. She is probably in the right job!

It would appear that this can all be put to bed, but Dave stated that the assessment would be in depth, interviewing our friends, our relatives, examining all aspects of our lives and that it would probably take up to 60 days due to the complexity of the case. This felt extremely invasive, judgemental and humiliating. Who would want their life to be examined in this manner? It felt like Big Brother gone mad. Apparently, this is unnecessary – it was an empty threat made to parents he took a dislike to. Or to correct that, a mother he took a dislike to. I failed the personality test. He wanted to tear our life apart because I disagreed with him, challenged his male ego, stood up to him. How dare I? So glad he no longer has any say in our lives, he felt like a dangerous, insidious being, looking to rip us apart.

I had to chase up the minutes of the TAC meeting he attended through the school. The minutes are as okay as they're ever going to be – however, some personal things were said, but he did not record them! He who writes the minutes holds the outcome of the meeting.

Diary: 25/11/15

I attended an autism conference yesterday at Stepping Hill and really struggled being around the "professionals". The question they all ask is, "Are you a professional or a parent?" Obviously, the two do not go together! They all arrive in packs of a least two – they cannot attend alone apparently! I have been all too aware that I need to discharge this anger and feeling of impotence and so I have been having EMDR.

Tomorrow, I am attending my third EMDR session. It is an interesting process. The client (me) talks about their issues and then I focus on the feeling. Then headphones deliver "clicking" sounds that move from ear to ear. I then follow the thoughts and feelings and the clicking is repeated. EMDR was developed to help with Post-Traumatic Stress

Disorders, but is not necessarily recommended for working with longer term issues, such as neglect, I have since found out. EMDR was one of the approved therapeutic interventions through the Post-Adoption Support Fund.

So far it has mainly involved history-taking. As the therapist, Liz, said last week, it involves going back into my history, a place in time that I have few clear memories about, if the truth be told. Is this selective or just poor memory? I am unsure. I am trying EMDR because of this feeling of anger (people keep saying it is, in fact, fear, but I disagree!). I wake up with a knot under my left breast that will not go away. Talking does not shift it. I am concerned as I do not want to feel like this anymore. I have had counselling, EMDR and I constantly challenge myself, trying to change my negative thinking. I am active, I have good friends and a supportive family – but still this knot continues.

I am fighting a system from the outside. I am powerless. No one is listening. I need people to do their jobs, but there are so many excuses to hide behind. There is no accountability. This is the reality I live in. This landscape will not change. *I need to change.* I still need to challenge the system and fight for Eric and my family, but I need to erect a wall to protect myself. I need to become more resilient.

This powerlessness triggers my feelings from when I was 15 and my dad left the family after having a tawdry affair. He drank too much, dabbled in drugs and crashed his car whilst under the influence. He had raging arguments with my mum and I had to intervene to protect my mum. I had never before stood up to my father before. He was a very bright man who came from nothing and worked his way up in Shell to become very successful – but that was not enough for him. He had no sense of self-worth, a poor childhood and shaky attachment foundations himself. Consequently, I lost a father who I admired. As the bricks fell around him, the weakness that was at his core was exposed. I had to confront a very stark new reality overnight. I lost a lot. I was powerless and remained so in the battlefield that became my parents' divorce. I was told too much and considered too little by both parents.

I felt this powerlessness again when Mum died after nine weeks in Wythenshawe hospital. I felt the same sense of unfairness. The staff were (bar a few) cruel and heartless. They questioned whether she was actually ill at all. The physiotherapists said she was "putting it on". She was dying in a hospital where there was no warmth for a fellow human being, a kind woman whose first thought was always, "What can I do to help?"

I think the situation with Eric triggers all of these feelings that lie dormant, but not discharged – and I want them discharged, spent. I want to reconcile the past and live in the here and now. I want to enjoy life, embrace opportunities, feel free and no longer be angry. I want to have peace.

Diary: 2/12/15

Still no contact or updates! Eric has gone onto a higher dose of Ritalin and is calmer at school by all accounts, but his behaviour at home is still very rude and challenging. Less so than in the past, but, even so, it is difficult to tolerate and manage. After the last meeting, the post-adoption worker was supposed to tell me about Non-Violent Resistance (NVR) because she had been on a course and it was fantastic, apparently. Anyway, no information has flowed this way as yet.

I bought the *Parents' Guide to the Response to Intervention* and have to say I am not impressed, but I did try a part of the approach. It recommends widening out the incidents of aggression to friends or family, who are willing to talk to the young person when things are going wrong at home. The thinking being that the person contacted reassures the young person that they are there for them, to support them. Few children rage at others as much as they do at parents. Apparently this is not shaming to the young person.

It also means that as a parent, you take the abuse, but do not react (I do this already and have done this for years) and then when all is calm, enter his room, block the doorway with your chair and ask for the child to come up with alternative strategies. Ask him to turn off the TV and so on and then just sit there for an hour.

I have now been for three EMDR sessions. The first two were establishing my issues. The third was actually working with the EMDR technique. The start of the third session entailed the counsellor saying that she did not know how she could actually help me as I seem to have reflected on my situation and resolved the issues.

I was a bit taken aback. I really wanted EMDR to help. I said that, even though I can rationalise my thought processes, I still feel anger. The feelings and frustration remain with me and fester. I said I'd like to change things, but, unfortunately, some things are beyond my control.

I had to describe my stress. I said it feels like a black hole in space. Spinning and sucking up all that is good and adding it to the toxicity that has become me. It sits under my left breast, heavy and dark. Black as black can be. Its depth is frightening. There is no bottom, no end to it. It is a force of nature, beyond my control.

I had headphones on and the clicking sounds were going from one ear to the other. I had to breathe in through my abdomen and let the air circulate to my lungs and fill my lungs. Then, when I could hold the breath no longer, I slowly released it through the abdomen again. This continued for several breaths. I then described my black hole. The process continued and then I looked at it again. By the end, the black hole was smaller and silver. More "egg on its side" shaped, less tumultuous. I did feel calmer strangely! Was it all just wishful thinking?

This week, I have tried to meditate. I find it challenging and have tried it before, but I am doing my homework! I have noticed that the black hole has not reappeared every time Eric has been rude. I have felt more in control and this must have an impact on him. Regardless of the front I have managed to portray, I am not congruent when dealing with him. The minute he starts his wind up to a full-blown challenge, my emotions go with him. My levels of stress usually going from 0 to 10 in a second. Now, I reach 0 to 6 and the chaos is less acute.

Diary: 7/12/15

A new phase? Okay, so the week started unfortunately: we had yet another meeting with the post-adoption social workers. We had met four weeks ago and the only contact we had since was late on Friday 4th December, in the form of an email regarding the Non-Violent Resistance information. There was no discussion of how it works, just a PDF. Bearing in mind that I had bought and read the book four weeks ago, this was hardly helpful. The meeting took place and the reason for the social worker not attending the assessment was due to a family crisis. Faye took full responsibility about not informing us. Surely, in the intervening four weeks, our post-adoption worker could have made contact in some shape or form?

The meeting was emotional again. Dermot has really disengaged and given up hope, I think. This was picked up on and the question, "What can be done to help you?" was asked several times. He just wants them out of our lives. As do I!

I felt so sad seeing him defeated by a system after 30 hard years in a job he hated. He endured it for the sake of our family, at much personal sacrifice. We adopted children to be good parents, to have a family and to give back to society – but Eric has all but blown us apart over 11 years, culminating in this travesty that is the allegation. It is the bell that cannot be un-rung, forever on our children's records, to be flagged up at all hospital admissions. Local Authority references will indicate that an allegation was made, affecting any possible future career options for Dermot. The implications are massive and underplayed by Social Services. The fallout is ongoing and forever taints the unblemished record of a good man.

The meeting covered a lot of ground, but will it change anything? No. Interestingly – and I do wonder if Faye realises this – (hopefully, because she is not a stupid woman) her actions from the previous meeting were all completed, but her colleagues' were not. Well, she had sent the NVR information through on the eve of the next meeting! Well done. All other issues, such as the psychologist's input, are still unresolved, although I still left the meeting not knowing what the problem is, other than the psychologist is now on maternity leave! It is 12 weeks since Dr. Pilkington's report was submitted to them and it lies in a drawer. EMDR has apparently died a death for Eric, even though I am going to try it for myself! Interventions are still zero! "Aiming High Breaks" are to continue in the short term. No concrete answers!

The real things that can help us are still left hanging in the balance. They are looking at Family Counselling with Sue Hawkins, the Educational Psychologist, and I feel that this may help us move on. Eric and Dermot need to rebuild their relationship and the family hopefully can move forward together, with some glue being applied by a skilled clinician. I hope it is Sue, as she is the only professional who to date has met Eric, assessed him accurately and submitted a helpful report. Fingers crossed!

The Family Support Worker did come yesterday. We have been waiting for this for four weeks! She seemed very nice and will work with Eric (after getting to know him) on anger, anxiety and self-esteem. Clearly, she does not have any training in this area, as she freely admitted, but, fortuitously, she is in an office on the same floor as the lead psychologist and is open to seeking help. Hopefully, it will help and, if it links in with school, Eric may learn to self-regulate and have someone to talk to, as he keeps asking for.

The meeting did at least show some desire to action things, but I still got sliced by various comments. When I said that I had got the NVR book myself, she said, "Well, you would, wouldn't you?" It seems that to be preemptive is a sin. The impression that precedes me is that of being a "know it all" and the fact that I research and enquire means that I am a threat. My curiosity is not an asset in this world that I am forced to inhabit.

Diary: 8/12/15

I had my EMDR today. I cried a lot. I had to think about the last difficulty I experienced, which was not

DIARY OF EVENTS FOLLOWING THE ALLEGATION

hard, as I used the meeting on Monday where I cried a lot again. I had clicking in my ears, going from one ear to the other, and Liz moved her two fingers in front of my eyes as I thought about the emotions. I then thought about Dermot and my sadness for him. We talked after each short clicking input and went with the next emotion and thought process. I went through Mum's death and the hospital and how badly she was treated. I ended up on my dad and the cruelty he showed to my mum at the time of their divorce when I was 15.

I realise that my focus is always drawn towards issues involving unkindness, lack of resolution and a failure to repair relationships. These things are my triggers, they are what I care about and what drive me to fight the system, to right wrongs!

I also explored the loss I feel personally. I have no identity outside of being Eric's stroppy parent: "That Woman". I have no real career, other than trying to help him and keep the family on an even keel. I do bits of counselling, which I love, but it does not cover my costs. I am not utilised enough. I love projects, I love being busy, and achieving change. I love to leave things in a better condition than I found them. I need to achieve things in order to feel validated and I suppose I do not feel that this will ever happen. My professional life stalled many years ago, probably when I was in the police, when I was on a trajectory that I chose to step off. All these years later, I still have not found the same recognition for my skills and abilities. At present, I am scrabbling around, working hard for no recognition or financial reward (and whilst money is not everything, it would help!). I do need an outlet! A channel to feel like all this has not been for nothing, but finding fulfilling roles is really a bit like searching for a unicorn – but maybe optimism can find me one of those along the way!

Diary: 9/12/15

My last EMDR was emotional, but, as Liz said, I slept more soundly last night than I have done in months! I do not feel particularly refreshed, but I did sleep! I genuinely feel that, in order for me to feel better, I need to effect a change. Something good has to come out of the mess we find ourselves in, whether this be in the form of help for other families or better service provision. To do this, reflective and reflexive practice needs to be ingrained in these institutions. I am not talking about line manager supervision. This is too close a relationship, where office prejudices becomes the lens through which the co-workers are perceived and dealt with. I think the relationship between colleagues is more important than addressing professional incompetence. Is a person going to give an honest account of themselves to their manager? Never! Is the manager skilled enough to see beyond the mask presented? Usually not.

So, systems need to change. Accountability must be achieved. Support for parents should be delivered in a timely manner. Counselling skills would benefit all concerned. Meetings should be chaired professionally. Agreements about chairs, agendas and minutes need to be agreed beforehand. All actions need to be allocated to a named person by a specific completion date on the minutes. Apologies need to be formally received, not just assumed, because if the parents failed to turn up, a great deal would be read into this – so equal playing fields would be beneficial.

Professionals also need to act as per their title and be humble. In many cases, they probably do not have as much experience as the parents, so they need to use empathy and know how to build relationships. They need to be kind and follow-up on their commitments and complete tasks in a timely manner. In short, they need to do what they are paid for.

Diary: 11/12/15

I have been wiped out this week. I think it is an accumulation of the meeting, the talk with the complaints department and the EMDR. The complaints people just want to write it off and the question is always the same, "What is it you want?" I want to feel better! I want to be heard and for lessons to be learnt. I accept that I cannot mend a broken system, but still I rail against it. Perhaps peace lies in no longer caring?

I have reflected on the meetings with Faye. She has afforded us time, but that is not to say that she has come to us without preconceptions. She seizes on phrases that I use and makes great play of the fact that I like to research and learn, but this is commented on in a way that is not a compliment! My enquiring mind is somewhat ridiculed. We were discussing Dialectical Behaviour Therapy (BDT), the "gold standard" of Cognitive Behavioural Therapy (CBT). I commented on the fact that it was originated by a female in the 1980s and her comment was, "You do feel it is important to recognise women …", the implication being that I am somewhat anti-men (hence the issues with Dave and Tim). The opposite could not be more true! I prefer male company on the whole and am comfortable in their presence. If anything I find women confusing!

Faye also has alluded to the fact that my manner can be annoying, but in a roundabout way because all her comments are veiled and cloaked in a light-hearted manner, but the meaning is clear. Even Dermot hears it. It is not worth addressing here, but nonetheless, it exists.

I have never been exposed to this problem before. Normally, the fact that you have a brain and can construct a reasoned argument works in your favour. The opposite is true in all my interactions with Social Services, Education and Health. I am truly at a loss in this world.

I would like to be seen by these professionals as an equal, with something to offer. Instead, they want me to shut up and go away. I would like to be held in high esteem, but realise, at the same time, that this will not happen. I suppose this is where a thick skin is necessary because each snub or rebuke cuts, wounding my psyche, tiring me out physically and mentally.

The upside of this week is that Sue Hawkins, the Educational Psychologist, will start to work therapeutically with our family in January. I like her as a professional, being one of the only professionals who has been able to see Eric as he is and work out what he needs. She "gets him" and I am hopeful that she will help us. We need to be more whole as a unit. Dermot must be able to move on and forgive being reported to the police. Healing is needed and new contracts established, new ways of being. The girls need to be heard. I am hopeful …

Ironically, considering all we've been through, this is now the calmest run-up to Christmas that we have ever experienced. The Ritalin is helping Eric and he is calmer and coping better at school, being more polite at home and more empathic than previously, even giving his older sister a hug when she was sad. I mean a real, genuine hug – it was lovely to see. Independent Options, who provide the one-to-one support for Eric, are brilliant (this is separate to the Tier 3 intervention that is short-term, when in crisis). He gets to go out with a helper on his own or in small groups of three or four young people. It gives us time to relax or just be with the girls. It is the first respite we have ever had and we just need it to continue.

Diary: 14/12/15

We had another TAC meeting today, run by the social worker now responsible for completing the assessment which remains open only until Short Breaks have finished a planned ending with Eric after Christmas. It seems they cannot work with young people unless there is a social worker allocated and that would no longer be the case because Eric is not at risk! So, she remains with us until after Christmas. Anyway, she took control of the meeting straightaway and it was clear we were not focusing on the past, but on moving forward.

There was positive input from Andy Ruddick (the Autistic Hub teacher at Castle Hill High School), who said there had been noticeable improvements in Eric's behaviour since joining the Hub and further movement since the medication. Eric is now in a position to learn! I fed back that this is the first time in our life with Eric that he is calm at this time of year. Previously, the months from September onwards just see an escalation in his behaviour to a pinnacle of vitriol that is impossible to cope with. For the first time, I can see empathy, humour and the ability to say, "Sorry". These are massive improvements! Hope is peeking through the ground.

Everyone at the meeting was respectful, just as a meeting should be. The agenda was Eric, as it should be. Progress … On the way out, we saw Mr. Law the headteacher, and he gave me a hug. This small gesture meant so much after the last few months. It felt that he was supportive and sorry for all that had gone on. Over this period, he was the only person (apart from Mr. Ruddick) who said anything kind and saw us as caring parents.

Again though, I have to say that the Social Services' Team Around the Child package means nothing. There was no attendance from CAHMS or Post-Adoption at this meeting (other than Cathy, the Family Support Worker). No apologies were offered, even though the meeting had been planned to accommodate the social worker's days off and part-time working. Professionalism around meetings seems to be non-existent.

Diary: 15/12/15

I have not been feeling great. I feel like I'm going down with something. I had to go to my professional supervision (a BACP requirement for all counsellors when in client contact) at 5pm that evening and really felt like going to sleep! I got there and Bev, my supervisor, said that she would no longer be supervising me due to personal matters. I did have some prior warning when her mum was diagnosed with a life-limiting illness and understood that she was making the right decision. I now need to find another supervisor with experience of working with young people.

I decided to seek accreditation with the BACP (a sign of experience in the counselling world) before Bev took her professional break, as she knew me well and could help with the process. The process of accreditation is quite onerous and Bev helped me to tailor my submission and was really helpful with this task.

I trained in order that I could use my hard-won knowledge through parenting Eric and researching best practice to help others. To hear anyone, especially young people, state that they wish to end their lives is a burden to carry. This is made even more difficult because there seems to be so little support elsewhere for these vulnerable individuals. My experience with Eric is mirrored with everyone else that I speak to. Adolescents, an extremely at risk group, fall between two stools when they reach 16 years old because they do not get picked up by adult services until they are 18. Who on earth thought that this was a good idea? The new structure that takes people from birth up until they are 25 years old makes more sense for everyone affected by SEN (Special Educational Needs).

Perhaps, now that things seem a bit calmer, I need to stretch myself more. Am I too old to start again, to try and establish myself in the world of work? I know that counselling is the right career path for me to pursue, but I just need to find my niche.

Diary: The New Year 2016

Christmas went surprisingly well! The "autistic wrist band" issued by the airport was a great success as it meant that, as a family, we could skip through baggage queues and security (were checked obviously!) and speedily board the plane, which reduced stress levels massively. What a brilliant scheme. Not all airports do it, unfortunately, but we did speak with the check-in people at Belfast and they afforded us the same courtesy. It's well worth remembering in future, as travelling with an autistic child is extremely stressful all round.

Being in Belfast with the relatives went well, but we probably outstayed our welcome by two days! Eric played computer games with his uncle most days, so he was very happy! The family do not really understand his issues – how could they? They had designed a lovely programme of events over the Christmas period, but we couldn't really adhere to it because, whilst this is okay for most children, it's not for Eric! He was rude to me most mornings and evenings, but significantly better than before.

We were back for one day and then off to the Lake District to my sister's holiday home. Eric was really calm and well-mannered and there are definite signs of him coping better with his anxiety. He even managed to sit through an hour of present unwrapping without having a meltdown. This, I am sure, is to do with the medication, but also school did a social story with him before the end of term about what to expect and how to behave which does seem to have helped.

Eric was looking forward to returning to school on the Tuesday, which is a miracle in itself. The only problem was that I had booked him in for a medication review on the Tuesday before school. In my mind, it made sense, but I failed to take his autistic brain into account. Well, he had a meltdown because seeing the GP and going back to school was all too much for him. It was really unpleasant and he called me names, but he did calm down eventually and even apologised! The next morning when he went to the GP and got taken into school, he was calm and cooperative.

He had a good first day back at school and saw Kathy, the post-adoption worker, for an hour that evening. He still hates going to bed and getting up and he has not made the connection between going to bed too late and being tired and hating to get up yet.

I felt quite off-colour for most of the holiday. The EMDR and/or the passage of time has helped me feel calmer and my chest is no longer a black hole, a vortex of unresolved emotion, and, whilst I did not sleep well last night, this is less of a common occurrence than before. Perhaps this is why I feel that I need a new purpose in my life as I am no longer fighting the system? We have as much help now as we are ever going to get for Eric and we have won some skirmishes, albeit at great personal cost. Maybe I am just feeling that sense of "what now?" I feel old and, at 51 years of age, I do not feel that I have a lot to show for all my hard work. Yes, I have a strong family, a good marriage, a nice home, two Springer spaniels and good friends. I have four buy-to-let properties and I have a lot of qualifications. But I lack direction …

18

THERAPY AT LAST!

Sue Hawkins, the Educational Psychologist who was employed by Stockport Post-Adoption, started working with our family after Christmas. Sue was the EP who assessed Eric in Year 6 and recommended that he really did need additional support – she seemed to understand him straightaway. Her first comments were that the most important thing to address was that the abuse Eric heaped upon us had to stop. For abuse it was. This was the first time that anybody had actually acknowledged what we're going through on a daily basis. It was a relief to feel heard, to be seen.

Just talking to Sue and feeling listened to was soothing. She suggested that we use elements of NVR to help, in that when Eric was angry, we would call up my sister, Elaine, or my friend, Clare, to speak to him in the role of mentor and friend. It had to be somebody who loved him and accepted him. The script was written and we actioned the plan. Initially, it did stop him in his tracks as he had to calm down to speak on the phone. The aim was to listen to him and to provide alternative solutions, different ways to dig himself out of the corner he had backed into.

On the first two occasions, this worked effectively, almost like a bucket of water shocking him into behaving, but, unfortunately, he then quickly worked out that all he had to do was refuse to pick up the phone or speak to the caller and his tantrum could go on as before. At least, it was a previously untried strategy and a new suggestion from an informed source whose judgement I trusted.

Sue spoke with Derm and myself, all the time acknowledging how difficult the allegation must have been for us all, but particularly for Derm. This in itself was helpful. The fact that she understood how we felt without us having to dredge everything back up again only for it to be left hanging, unresolved or misunderstood by the other party was incredible for us. I felt for the first time in years, since Lynne from MAS retired, that we had someone who was looking at our family holistically and with kindness.

Sue mentioned that she had just completed a course on a new type of therapy called Lifespan Integration Therapy (LI) and wondered about using it for Eric. This was the first time that therapy for him had actually been mentioned. Previously, attachment issues were viewed as being untreatable, a condition for life. People could work around them and – as one of the workers from Derbyshire CAMHS stated many years ago – visit them in borstal.

Sue sounded a bit tenuous when suggesting it: the therapy for attachment repair works with the individual using the timeline of their life and two or three specific memories per year. The therapist holds a "baby" and mirrors attachment and love. She was unsure about how a 13-14 year old boy would respond to this, but I was clear that we should give a go. In the first session that she was to work with Eric, he decided to not come out of his room because he'd had a bad day at school. We left it and she came the next week and Eric did come out of his room. Sue had arrived with a paper bag with a "baby" (doll) dressed in a Manchester City kit – Eric is passionate about Manchester City!

The therapy involves using your imagination and seeing what a secure attachment would have looked like. Eric took part quite happily in the process and found it relaxing. The therapy rebuilds new neural pathways that would have developed in a securely attached child. The neurons develop and "knit" over the next 24 hours and, in fact, the following weeks can be marked by changed beliefs about self and increase feelings of security.

Eric did change. He showed definite signs of feeling more secure. He was less anxious, less angry and more empathic. Yes, other changes had occurred in his world too, such as him having become part of the Hub for autistic children where they understood and helped him cope in a joined-up manner between home and school, plus he was now on medication for his ADHD. The allegation he made had been resolved and put to bed and Derm was calmer with him and able to manage his behaviour in an increasingly non-inflammatory manner.

But, in essence, the Lifespan Integration therapy was having a massive impact on Eric and our environment at home. I honestly do not believe that any real progress would have been made by Eric if not for LI – his environment may have adapted to meet his needs and manage his behaviour, but he would not have learnt how to do this for himself. As Sue said, talking therapy could not shift this internal belief system, the cellular feeling of being unloved and unlovable, of feeling chaotic and fear-driven.

Things began to feel calmer for and around Eric. We were having the occasional challenge, but it was short-lived. He would disappear off and then reconnect afterwards. Our holiday to the Lake District for half-term in May 2016 got off to bad start as Eric's tantrum started that first Sunday night. The abuse was unpleasant, but Eric did eventually go to bed, but not before calling me all the names under the sun. The girls had left the living room in disgust at Eric's behaviour, but crept down later to offer me a hot chocolate to help me feel better and Derm also found the Cadbury's Fingers! (There is a theme here! Mum likes chocolate and uses it to self-soothe and self-medicate!)

That evening Derm and I debated why we bother with holidays at all, as this behaviour is a common issue. However, the alternative, to stay home, fills me with dread. Holidays, even after 12 years of Eric's aversion therapy, are better than staying at home. Home means to feel trapped – trapped by domestic boredom: all I can see are windows that I wash, but then look appalling when the sun shines on them. I am not a good housewife!

The rest of the week went well with Eric. He even elected to stay in the Lakes with me instead of going home a little earlier with Derm, as the girls had work and athletics meets to attend. My niece stayed as well and although, when all four children are together, Eric is left out, when the girls are out of the picture, they are really kind and considerate to each other. They are good friends.

This improvement in Eric being able to self-regulate is a new thing and one that I am sure is linked with LI therapy. For the first time in over 11 years, I could see and feel a fundamental shift. Hope began to emerge for all of us!

The moles …

The irony is that whilst Eric was appearing calmer, my eldest daughter lost the plot! I have often described having three adopted children as being like playing a game of "Whack a Mole" – the aim to be to hit the mole over the head so that no heads are above ground.

Obviously, I do not mean this literally, but when one child is calmer, the others become somewhat "unglued".

Jess has always seemed to be more "sorted" than Eric. She is the happy child with luminous red hair, who can light up a room. She has, in the past, been kind with Eric and looked out for him. This all changed at Easter 2016. Jess had achieved far more in her GCSEs than we had anticipated and she was able to go to Loreto College to study for a P.E. BTEC Level 3 Extended Diploma, which was her first choice of college. Jess was now 17 years-old. She battled through the winter and certainly struggled with the travelling that was taking her about 90 minutes each way. Derm picked her up on her half-days and he helped where he could. We gave her more freedom too: she had an iPad, a phone with connectivity and she began to spend more and more time in her room, isolating herself.

We put this behaviour down to being a teenager and part of the necessary separation between parent and child as they move towards independence. We realised that there were common themes of lying about where she was going and who she was seeing, which were imprinted by her first boyfriend when she was 14. Jess knew we disliked him (he had dumped her and devastated her) – he wanted to be friends with benefits. We didn't mind the friends bit ...

We saw that when a boy was on the scene, Jess always "disappeared". She closed down and headed for the cliff edge, oblivious to what may well lay ahead. All through our years together, I had therapeutically parented her, talked her through cause and effect and encouraged communication with her, the underlying message being that you get in more trouble for lying than for the actual misdemeanour. I hope I instilled in her that no act is too great to repair. With acknowledgement comes learning and that no one is perfect. Falling down is fine – just get up again, learn and move forwards. I used all the tools in my extensive repertoire to try and educate Jess in her actions and choices and how she should truly value herself. It was like talking to a wall. Nothing stuck.

It is like we have not been there ourselves. Jess has always "shut down" and gone "off-line" when in trouble, desperate to be the good girl. If I compliment anyone else, she always looks slightly peeved, as if by recognising another's worth, I am criticising her and finding her wanting. She has always liked to be "seen", to pour out to adults every single new thing she has done or achieved. The accolades have never been enough for her because she does not feel worthy.

This shutting down has occurred since she was two-and-a-half and probably before. As a two-year old, she appeared to be depressed. She did not know how to play with toys when she came to live with us in the June of 2001. If she was told off, the shutters fell and her large brown eyes gazed out with nothing behind them. This look is reminiscent of the Romanian orphans that were on the news a number of years ago, gazing out from behind the bars of their cots with dead eyes, lost in pain.

As she grew older, these occasions became less, but were always in the background.

Jess never really admitted to anything she had done and I am sure that other children have been blamed for things that she was responsible for in the past, but we thought that she was the one least likely to be naughty. Only recently we found out that some damage that was done to a holiday home in Anglesey (not massive, but taking plaster off a patch of wall that required remedial action), was Jess, not the others. How easily fooled were we! The others were punished, but she did not come forward. Interestingly, Eric, although only six, came forward to take the blame to stop everyone getting into trouble.

There were early signs of Jess falling too deeply for ill-intentioned boys. At school, her first boyfriend claimed she was clingy and then continued to pick her up and drop her at will. Following the prom in June 2015, a young man commented how pretty she looked (which she did!) and, suddenly, it was a big love affair again. This did not last long, but, tragically, some months later he died unexpectedly. Jess was devastated.

From her birthday in January 2016, Jess started to shut down and turned away from us all. She spent all her time in her bedroom and, whilst I know that this is not unusual for teenagers, for her it was different. We knew that the transition to college had been hard for her, but she had opted to go to Loreto, which is in the middle of Hulme. The college was only six miles from home, but took 1.5 hours each way on public transport. She battled with this all through the winter, never complaining. Jess told us of an incident at Piccadilly station where a drunk had approached and frightened her and she talked of being shoved around when trying to get on the bus home, but the depth of her unhappiness was not disclosed. Jess then had another boyfriend, but the relationship didn't last long. However, her grief was disproportionate to the length of the relationship.

We became concerned about the time she spent on the phone and about her withdrawal from the family. I talked to her and tried to be as open as possible, but she was "off-line". Nothing was reaching her and she was becoming more moody, more remote, more lost. I was increasingly scared for her. I asked for Sue to work with her and do the Lifespan Integration Therapy for her as well because talking was not effective. The intervention was agreed, but took over three months to materialise.

The reason for the delay was that Sue had not yet finished working with Eric and I did not want him to be left high and dry. Sue is overworked and her department has not got enough staff. The funding was coming via the Post-Adoption Fund and assessments had to be updated. This bureaucratic necessity took time and the social worker involved wanted to delay it further as she wanted to meet with Jess and Sue at the same time. In fact, the social worker had already met with Jess and I felt as though she was just adding another layer of bureaucracy to the process. I contacted her manager who agreed that the work was a continuation, rather than a new piece requiring a full report, which I felt was a common sense approach.

LI Therapy for Jess started in July 2016. In the meantime, we had tried to keep her safe. We thought that the promise of removing her from college if she did not improve would be a wake-up call and make her realise how serious things had become. We thought she would want to stay, but the opposite was true! She practically bit our hands off, so, after the Easter holiday, she remained at home. We found a new course at Cheadle College for her starting in September, a college she could easily walk to. Jess said that she felt safer being closer to me. We helped her learn to drive and cared for her, but we found out that she was still a lost child, unable to tell us how she felt or identify what she needed.

Jess just ploughed her own furrow, not talking, sulking, becoming angry during any communication. This was so out of character for our previously bubbly, exuberant child, but more salient was the fact that she was unable to see the risks she was taking with her psyche and her future. Jess was deeply unhappy, but was unable to emerge from her depression by herself. Talking saw no movement emotionally or developmentally in all of the weeks spent at home with us around her. For us, it was like Groundhog Day with no hope showing through.

When I looked at her, I saw dissociation. This child/woman was diametrically opposed to the daughter that we have held close and loved unreservedly. Developmentally,

I am well aware of the need for a teen to separate from their parents in order to grow up. I could cope with a healthy separation that reflected normal teenage maturity – it was not about trying to stop her becoming independent, but about her keeping herself safe and making informed life choices. She was depressed and lonely, even though she did not recognise it. The hope was that Sue Hawkins could effect change through LI.

We have come to the conclusion that Jess is more "damaged" than we first believed. Her dissociation is an indication of a deeper neglect or abuse than we ever were informed about. We will probably never know what happened to our daughter. We now realise that she seems unable to form deep relationships – she has a friend, but forgets to contact her! We thought she was a social butterfly, befriending many, but closer inspection demonstrates that she cannot communicate unless it is about herself.

She does not really have any interest in others; she feels deeply for herself, but struggles with the feelings of others. Jess does not know how to have a "real" relationship and is afraid to try. Jess had always been the outgoing, confident child. She was bright and lovely to be around. This change in her was dramatic and showed how deeply early trauma is embedded in the DNA of the afflicted person. Jess was definitely demonstrating attachment issues because of her adoption and fractures in her feelings of security that were hidden by her outward demeanour and probably masked from our consciousness by our preoccupation with Eric and his explosive behaviour. I felt guilty for missing the signs, for not helping sooner.

Diary: 28/06/16

Jess is distant and looks at me with dead eyes, coupled with a flash of hatred. I am the villain of the piece and her dad is the "good parent". I fear that this year will forever separate me from my daughter, that I will lose her. To her, I will always be the one who judged and took everything from her, the one who does not want her to have a boyfriend. She is not wrong, I am. Sue Hawkins (and her sister, Zoe) feel that she does not like the fact that I have exposed her darker side, the side that she does not wish to own.

Two children live within the same body and neither likes the other. So still we sit and endure, waiting for help. Hoping for some movement, for Jess to start to love herself and value herself, just as we do. I feel that I am holding my breath, hoping for miracles where none may exist. I am pinning my hopes on Sue and a therapy that I feel is too good to be true! I feel faintly ridiculous and somewhat naïve at the thought, but the other options are too bleak – to accept the loss of a child because the road she is on will not end well. These early forays into womanhood set the scene for her future relationships and concept of self-worth. I want better for her and if I have to be the "bad guy", then so be it, because someone has to. She is worth fighting for.

Sue met with her last week (w/c 21/6/16) and discussed therapy. She put her mind at rest that she does not have to dwell or reveal her issues or sense of shame. Sue will start with relaxation and then continue at a pace that suits Jess.

Unfortunately, the next time Sue comes, the post-adoption worker will come too. Why, I don't know. The extra hours have been agreed for Jess, but I feel angry with the delay. I do not want the therapeutic time to be taken up with a paper-pusher trying to insert themselves into a process where they have no role. I just want the therapy to actually start.

Rightly or wrongly, my experience of the post-adoption workers is that they are just scribes, custodians of the gateway that allows access to the land of funding. Not once since we asked for help, other than a home visit, have we been contacted to see how things are, how Jess is. If I needed their support, I would have been left hanging.

19

NEW INSPIRATION

The Lifespan Integration Course Stage 1

I attended the Stage 1 Training for Lifespan Integration on 10th & 11th June 2016 in Crawley. I did not even know where Crawley was – needless to say, it is a long way from Manchester: four train changes away, in fact! I stayed in Crawley with my sister on the Thursday night in the Travelodge. It transpires that I was 1.6 miles away from the venue, so I decide to walk, following the map I had printed out. I went the wrong way! I walked and ran over five miles and turned up five minutes late, in a sweaty heap. Five minutes late is not significant to most, but I am always early!

I usually attend courses and come away feeling dissatisfied with the input and usually feel that I have not learnt anything of any use, often feeling that I know more than the trainers. Similarly, I am wary of the course participants as I have not always found this world of therapy to be particularly welcoming and I have found some people quite closed and judgemental.

However, this course was a very different experience for me. I came away lighter and looking forward to seeing the participants again. I liked the trainers and felt that they had much to teach me. The course started with explaining the process of LI and the neurological impact of memories on the body. It all made sense to me. One other participant was sceptical but valued the opinion of the consultant who had recommended the course to her. I felt it was worth trusting the training.

We watched an LI protocol in the round with a volunteer. The experience was moving to watch for us and also for the volunteer. It did not feel voyeuristic or intrusive. We later divided into triads and took turns as client, therapist and observer. I was the client initially. I explored an event from when I was 15, when my dad left. I explored the memory and felt okay to end as the body-held feeling had left my core.

On reflection, after Day 1 of the course, I realised that I felt peaceful and not upset by the process. I had cried, but it felt more like tears of compassion were flowing, rather than that I was emotional. It felt gentle.

The following day, I inadvertently volunteered to be the client in front of the group. Mandy, the trainer, asked for anyone who had a secure attachment history. I said that I had and, without thinking, I had volunteered! The process involved Mandy holding a life-like doll and speaking to "her" as if she were my "baby" self. I was asked to look at her and then go to a calm place in my head. I kept seeing Mandy being replaced by the image of my mum and I felt warmth down my back. Tears flowed again, but it was not in sadness. I did not feel exposed, even though I was in front of 20 people that I did not really know.

That afternoon saw me being the therapist. My client was a very nice man who had really struggled with the whole LI process as it was similar, but markedly different to, the system he used and believed in, Family Systems Integration. He struggled with the concept of integrating the younger self with the adult self and I believed that he saw it as assimilation rather than integration, where the parts are separate, but communicate as a whole.

He struggled to find a source memory as he was too cognitive and found it difficult to access his right brain. We then opted to look at an issue that he had that was unresolved. The somatic feeling was hard and under his breast at the start, but, by the end, it had begun to "float like feathers" outside his body. He was perplexed and felt that he needed time to process what had occurred for him in the session.

I left the training feeling very optimistic and that I had a new tool that could alter my practice. I had already identified several people I was working with, who were "stuck" and not progressing as I would have expected. I spoke to them all the week after the training and, having got their agreement, asked them to do the timeline and bring it with them.

On Tuesday 21st June 2016, I worked with a female client. We explored the somatic feeling initially and found that it was heavy and in her core. After the session, she described the feeling as being lighter and that she could look at the issue she brought to the session and laugh at it, seeing it as a normal sibling problem.

My second client was 13 years old. Her issue presented in the chest and under her breast. At the end, she felt calmer and the feeling had had left her body. This was from someone who had presented as being riddled with anxiety and fear. It was the first positive move for this client.

Interestingly, I had worked at the Secondary School that day, seeing five students and then two private clients. Normally, I feel tired and drained at the end of this as counselling involves complete absorption in the client for the full hour. That evening, however, I felt light and re-energised. I met with two friends for dinner at the local Indian restaurant and felt relaxed and awake!

I do feel a bit sceptical because I wonder if it is all a bit too simple and that perhaps I have been taken in by something. I hope not, but only time will tell! I had felt the benefit of EMDR myself, but having researched it further in relation to attachment issues, I had mixed feelings. LI, however, actually appears to heal attachment and it is gentle. I love it. I want to become more experienced and skilled in its use and I can see a direction for me in my therapeutic practice, a direction that I have been seeking for a long time. LI seems to provide a greater impact than other therapies that I have learnt about.

The Lifespan Integration Course Stage 2

Diary: 20/10/16

I have just caught the train to Oxford for the second part of the LI training. This means that I can advertise on their website as opposed to just being able to use it in practice. My thoughts are that I really like the therapy, but I recognise that it is relatively unknown in the UK. It is well-established in the USA, but has failed to launch fully over here. I want to base my practice on LI, but know I need to have a market for it.

I need to have a vision for my future practice. The sixth form where I love working – the students are consistently fascinating to work with – may use a larger counselling provider in the near future, in line with the main school. This means that I may not be employed by them in the next academic year.

Working with young people is both massively rewarding, but also onerous because of all of the necessary safeguarding issues. The safety of clients is of paramount importance and I am completely in agreement with this or I would not do this job, however, it basically means that there are restrictions on the level of confidentially afforded to the students. Anything can be deemed as being a safeguarding issue. When their confessions are exposed, a whole new momentum takes over: safeguarding officers become involved, parents are contacted, GPs enlisted, then there are referrals to CAMHS or the equivalent and, depending on the issue, even the police. It seems to talk too openly can result in the very thing they most feared – everyone becoming involved, worried and interfering with their lives.

I have a jaded opinion of people being brought into the criminal arena as a victim. In no way do I believe the perpetrators deserve to go free, but experience has shown me that the victim is usually the one on trial, savaged by the defence, their peers and often abandoned by their parents as relationships falter in the face of the young person not being believed or, at least, feeling that this is the case. The victim is re-victimised all over again.

However, I now realise that I need to get on with developing myself and a new pathway, which may or not involve counselling in schools. Writing seems to make sense and hopefully LI will show me a way forward? I attended the two-day course and found it interesting once again. The other participants were a mix of familiar faces from the previous course and new attendees to me, at least. The mix of individuals was a positive one, once again.

The training revisited some of the learning from Stage 1 – acting as a refresher, which was useful. We also saw quite a few video sessions conducted by Peggy Pace, showing her work with dissociative clients. The work was powerful and reaffirmed to me that LI is an amazing tool therapeutically. The transformation of the individuals was staggering. My only criticism was that the recordings were many years old and some of the protocols displayed had altered in the intervening years. For example, the therapist now holds the doll during the Attunement Protocol, rather than the client.

I left feeling ready to take the therapy forward, but remain unsure how this is going to happen. As I mentioned previously, LI is not widely known in the UK, and, therefore, clients do not know to look for it! Mandy and Natasha, the course facilitators asked for volunteers to become involved in LI in the UK, as they would both be retiring in 2017. I did not rush to volunteer, but gave it some considerable thought on the journey home. I think I will volunteer because if the mantle of LI is not picked up, then it will surely die a death in the UK – you know me, always fighting for the cause! I am not concerned as to whether I am part of the organisation or if others become involved, but I am sure that I want to see it become part of the body of well-known therapeutic interventions for attachment and trauma. I would like to see LI become mainstream.

20

THE MOLES IN OCTOBER

Jess broke her leg just before starting Cheadle College, so certainly she would not be able to slip under the radar now – but she has not moaned at all, she's just got with it. Sue Hawkins has got two more sessions with her following our talk last week. I am noticing a change, but am wary of hoping that we have Jess back. She does seem happier, more relaxed, and is even coming downstairs more and is watching a box set called *Blindspot* with me most evenings. She has friends at college and is maintaining her long-term friendship with Beth, which I am really pleased about – as is she! They went to see Jake Bugg at the Apollo last night and loved it, just the girls, no adults! I did not worry at all, which is a massive change, a release that I have not had since Easter, when we first realised that she had collapsed.

Many changes have occurred for Jess: she has changed college and now goes to Cheadle College, walking the distance from home. She changed courses from BTEC Level 3 Diploma in P.E. to Health & Social Care. The teachers know her and she likes them enough to ask for clarification about learning issues. She has friends. She is beginning to like herself! But I do believe that she could not have embraced these changes without LI changing her neurological pathways. Talking did not shift her at all and I am good at talking!

Sue and others have noticed the changes and this reinforces that I am not just clutching at straws. The last two sessions with Sue are imminent and then Sue will work with Eric again. Eric has been the best he has ever been in a new term, but he has also let himself down in some big ways!

Last week, the girls told Derm that Eric was smoking in our bathroom. I hate smoking with a passion. My best friend died of lung cancer and when I visited him at Christies, his only regret was that he had smoked and, thereby, shortened his life by at least 10 years. Ann, his wife, is still with us, but, due to smoking, she has COPD (Chronic Obstructive Pulmonary Disease) and is on heavy-duty inhalers. I hate the smell and the lack of consideration for non-smokers. Anyway, I hate smoking and also, where was the money coming from for Eric to buy cigarettes? I contacted the school and found out that they were aware of a young man "giving" cigarettes to the pupils and they were sorting it out. At least he was not stealing from my purse! But he could have set fire to the house as he was dumping his "dimps" and matches out of the bathroom window onto the roof below. He will not have thought about the risks concerned.

I have to admit that this behaviour made me feel like we were back to square one. I was disappointed, tired and angry, but this was soon countered by some good news: that that very week he received a postcard home from school, congratulating him on his efforts in P.E., for being a top football player in KS 3 & 4 and he had been elected onto the School Council for the year! Thus, he did earn back his treats for the weekend, most notably playing football in a competition with Manchester City's Disability group on the Friday and he watched Stockport County no less, together with Jess, Derm, Beth and her dad. This indicates that although his path may never be smooth, he is on an upward trajectory.

Eric's behaviour is still volatile, but the anger lasts for a far shorter time. He can bring himself down most of the time. Even when caught out about the smoking, he was unhappy and a bit cross, but normally this would have resulted in a major incident lasting for hours and hours – this time it blew over pretty quickly. This is change indeed.

The next LI work with Eric is going to look at helping him further with his anxiety and his friendships, as this is still a struggle. Having said that, his current "nemesis" from the Hub is not mentioned every day and he does not seem to be getting into arguments daily, as he was before. Normally, the target of his anger and anxiety will then become a "friend", but another adversary will take his place as the perpetrator of all wrongs, the person to blame and rail against every day and talk about incessantly. Eric has always sought out an adversary and has always gone from one to another in a series of friends/foes/enemies. It seemed he felt friendships were begat in this manner and he knew no other way of bonding with his peers, so this more relaxed attitude to his friends is a new development.

Diary: 21/10/16

I came back from the LI course straight into half-term. We went up to the Lakes to my sister's lovely second house in Flookburgh. The transition of me rejoining the family and going on holiday went amazingly well.

Eric was exceptionally good all week, except for a couple of minor blips over computer usage (as usual). The first happened at bedtime, but he did surrender the computer before bed, albeit muttering at me for some time, but, in the morning, without prompting, he apologised for his behaviour. The second incident occurred on our return home. Eric took the computer to bed and did not want to give it back. He huffed and puffed, but did give it to me, throwing it into my suitcase, but even this behaviour is significantly better than normal.

Derm and the girls returned home and Eric and I spent a day and night together on our own, whilst waiting for Elaine and Naomi to arrive from London. I was a bit concerned about how this would go, but we had a really peaceful time. We walked Pearl (our Springer spaniel – sadly, Sophie, our older Springer died in 2016) to Cartmel and had a pub lunch at his request (the pub lunch, not the walk!). He talked all the way there, but in a calm manner, making conversation. This was probably the best time we have had together since … well, ever? It feels this way anyway.

On our return home, we found that Zoe was not in a happy place. She had been having online conflict with the boyfriend of her old best friend. The friendship had ended last summer, with Zoe being unceremoniously ejected from the position of being the "best friend". Her ex-friend wrote a list online, putting her friends in order of import and Zoe barely figured. This was hurtful and not subtle! This information was then aired to all and sundry and the end of the friendship was not Zoe's choice. Zoe has not been unkind about this girl – indeed, she feels sorry for her as she knows that she is going through issues at home as her parents are splitting up.

I do not get why the boyfriend is involving himself and making things worse, but, equally, I would just block him from all social media accounts. This, of course, is too hard for a teenager to work out! The sadness for me is the fact that Zoe feels unable to confide in me. She will tell her sister, her brother and even her cousin before me – though, that's quite normal for teens and mums, I suppose. The route for me to find out there were problems went via London and back to me, as opposed to from her bedroom to the lounge downstairs!

I know she is stressed as she is finding the BTEC Level 3 Extended Diploma in Art & Design challenging, but, again, she will not accept help from me, insisting that if she needs help she will ask the college for it. I am not sure she will. She is also trying to resit her English GCSE after getting a D in the summer. Nowadays, young people have to get their English and Maths before being able to do anything else. This is a major hurdle for a lot of young people, especially if, like Zoe, you have dyslexia that was only diagnosed in Year 11. The stress in Zoe is demonstrated by her being quieter than normal and somewhat surly!

I have since found out that she has "friended" her birth dad on Facebook, going against all advice from ourselves and the social workers. She had her fingers burnt in the summer when her elder brother was threatening suicide whilst she was on NCS (National Citizens Service – a government-run youth development scheme, which is really good!) and away from home for four nights. She panicked and I had a call from the on-duty manager. We decided it was best to confiscate all gadgets in the evening as we wanted to reinforce that this was not the agreed means of communication. It was agreed with Social Services that the girls could only write letters to their older siblings because both their brother and sister were not in a great place emotionally and direct contact may be detrimental to all of the children. I agreed that I would see that they were given to the relevant department.

I did ring the Darlington on-call social worker to get help for Zoe and Jessica's brother after the suicide cry for help via Facebook. They told me to ring the police. I disagreed strongly and firmly told them that I was telling *them* and that they could access records as to his whereabouts in the northeast. I had no information as to where he would be and felt that this was their responsibility. The on-call social worker was very unpleasant and obviously wanted to take no responsibility for the issues raised, but, as a member of the public, living in the Northwest, I felt that I had no authority to get anything done. It just added to my frustration with Social Services – the fact that they took no responsibility and were happy to leave the dilemma with me.

The upshot is that Zoe is continuing to do as she pleases and will not take advice, no matter how well-meant. She is obviously seeking some connection outside of her adopted family, which is natural. At the present time, Jess likes to hear about her siblings, but does not directly seek contact through social media. I understand this all too well, but it does hurt. Yes, it truly does! You go into adoption knowing that the children have a family out there and you keep the agreed contact, even when Social Services have disappeared. However, the pull of the birth family is always there – tugging at them towards their past, an inextricable bond that surpasses all you do for a child that you love beyond any reason. The child you have comforted, protected, looked after when ill, supported and loved unconditionally, still sees their birth family as this magical oasis of love and belonging.

Adopting means that you are always the second-best family, the "also ran", the one that they have had to live with and put up with, when really they want to return to their "real" mum and dad. Adopters are the surrogates, the make-doers, the ones who have to be there, but are never as important as the ones that got away. This pain can never be fully appreciated by natural parents. You can be the best parent possible and still be unimportant to your child, a stop-gap until true belonging and happiness can be re-established. The birth family are the heroes, the king and queen in the story. Even though they were unable to parent (and Social Services do not remove children lightly) or keep them safe, they are still perfect in their child's eyes. Zoe's parents left their older son wandering on a railway line; their eldest daughter fell off the settee fracturing her skull; they were sent to school with untreated burns on their feet from playing with scalding water; they were neglected – but the parents remain frozen in time as perfect figures who were stopped from being there by outside forces.

In fact, contact was supposed to continue when the girls were placed with us, but the birth parents kept letting their children down, repeatedly failing to turn up for the appointments with their children. Contact was stopped in the best interests of the children. Derm and I met the parents once and, to be honest, they seemed a bit "slow", asking superficial questions about the food the girls ate. They did not seem distraught or unhappy or guilty, just quite disinterested. To my knowledge, they never collected any of our letterbox contact letters that I sent for years, informing them about the girls' progress. The image of the birth parents is a projection of perfection, of what might have been. And, yes, it still wounds.

The counselling Zoe has been receiving at Central Youth is due to end after 12 sessions, but I doubt that there has been any impact for her. She says that she does not know if it has helped and I see no evidence of change. I think she needs LI too! I know that I make a real difference for the young people I counsel, so why can Zoe not receive the same help?

Sue Hawkins has finished LI therapy with Jess now and she seems more like our old Jess. She is chatting more and more able to say how she feels. She is dressing better – more like her age, whereas before she dressed like a seven-year old who had found a dressing-up box and was madly experimenting! She mixed colours and styles and looked as if she did not really care. She left her hair messy and did not wear make-up, but now she is making far more effort and she looks lovely. She seems sunny again. I need to say as well that she drove to and from the Lakes with her dad in the passenger seat, which I think is amazing! No fear – off she goes in the little car!

As agreed, Sue is now starting to work with Eric again. I am pleased as he has identified some areas that he feels would be beneficial, including helping with anxiety and friendships. I am looking forward to her starting with him again, as her work with him was curtailed before the summer due to Jess descending into an abyss. I am also aware that Sue's work with us will end soon. This leaves me feeling somewhat vulnerable, unsettled and questioning – do we need more help or are we on the up?

And things were going so well!

Diary: 10/11/16

Things were going so well – although "well" is a relative term in the context of our family. Last night went okay as Eric watched his team, Manchester City, beat Barcelona. All was good other than he was concerned because a boy from school said that Eric's only friend, "hated him". I reassured him that was unlikely and that he should contact his friend himself.

This morning, a boy possessed emerged from his pit of a bedroom, two minutes prior to leaving for his taxi, unwashed, unclean and in foul temper. When asked if he had at least done his teeth, the abuse started. It started off with a torrent of swearing and culminated in F-off gestures, the C word, and so on. It was a veritable tirade of abuse and all before 8a.m.. How can such a short period of time escalate into such devastation?

As he left, I was feeling angry, abused, distraught. I tried to access my emails before leaving for work (counselling teens in a college – ironic, or what?) and was unable to log in. Jess had been on the computer. I asked her, not all that calmly, why I couldn't get onto my email. She looked at the floor as if I was about to thrash her. I explained that I was upset and that this was about me feeling abused, not about her. Had she been in the wrong? No.

I offered to drop the girls off at college on my way past, but Jess did not get that my mood was not about her. Zoe, surprisingly, just gave me a heartfelt hug. How strange that she knew what I needed and yet I never know what she needs?

Derm had just got back from the doctor, only to be met by chaos, saying, "I only left 15 minutes ago!" He hugged me and said I should have said what a judge said to a defendant in court recently: on being called the C word, she replied, "You are a bit of a C yourself!"

Having been in the police, it is not the first time I have been called this, but, as I said to Derm, the upset comes from it happening in my home, by my son and feeling powerless to stop his abusive behaviour. On top of this is the feeling of going backwards because I had begun to believe that the abusive Eric was in the past. It feels like a smack in the face on many levels.

The additional stressors were that I had to take the girls to college, aware that Jess was feeling sorry for herself and I hate to see her feeling stressed, but I was unable to make things better before she went into college. I was also aware that I was upset that she was making it all about her when I was the one who had been verbally abused. I was the one needing support and comfort.

Also, I then had to arrive at the 6th Form College ready for counselling six young people, one after the other. I had to stop crying and hope my eyes were not red, my mascara not running in rivulets down my face. I put my game face on, empathy on tap. I think the isolation of life as an adoptive mother comes home at times like this – there is no one to call who can really see the path I travel.

As a counsellor, I am on my own. I cannot share my morning's tribulations with people at the school because the work is confidential and, anyway, I have no peers in this environment. I am the counsellor, the holder of pain and secrets. I should not be someone who needs support.

I need to find a team! I have contacted a few counsellors in my area to set up a peer supervision group and they have (rudely, I think) not answered me! But I will carry on as someone may want to join up, even if only to save money on supervision costs.

Diary: 5/12/16

I did re-group and held my first peer group supervision! Only one person turned up, but the other interested party did have a genuine reason for not being able to come. The counsellor who came seemed really nice and is seeking the same sort of help as I am: support; sharing of ideas; CPD (Continuing Professional Development).

Interestingly, she works within the adoption support area, so we have a lot in common. So things are boding well for the New Year and this will help with my feelings of isolation and supervision costs!

I did try and set up a peer support group for LI in my area, but have not received any interest. A similar get together is planned in the south. I also contacted two other LI practitioners in Sheffield and sought a meeting. I have to admit to being disappointed that they were too busy to meet even via Skype. I feel that for LI to embed in the UK, it needs to be properly promoted. I believe that some more people are involved in LI UK organisation, but my services are not required. I am a little disappointed, but, after some reflection, I have realised that I do not actually mind. As long as the therapy is rolled-out and becomes more high profile, then I am happy. Perhaps to become involved in this organisation may have been too much of a commitment for me – and I am perhaps too opinionated to be wanted in the fold! I am aware that I do challenge and want things to move forward at a pace that others may not always be happy with. Maybe the universe is telling me that I am not meant to be part of an organisation, that perhaps I am meant to set up on my own, diversifying from just counselling into another, connected area? This may be adoption or LI-focused or the two combined.

Derm and myself attended a meeting recently regarding the Regional Adoption Agencies (RAA).

The meeting updated us on how the reconfiguration of the service was going. The government-led changes were introduced in June 2015, but the changes to date (December 2016) are limited in their innovations. I wrote an article earlier this year (that unfortunately went unpublished) about the reorganisation and my concerns have to date been sadly realised. The only change is that a new tier of management has been added. The government provided funding for a consultant to aid the process and I believe that this has been provided through Adoption UK. They are seeking further funding through representation of adopters at the board level to help drive the process through.

As I said, the innovations are limited. The basis for arranged operations and new systems to measure success are in the pipeline, but the ground support services remain constant. Adoption support is still to be provided by social workers, most of whom work part-time. My belief is that some of the work – not the formal assessments that require statutory assessment – could be better provided by counsellors, experienced adopters or psychologists. I feel that a mentoring system could benefit adopters at all stages of the adoption process and imaginative provision could provide more support, cost-effectively.

There is a further meeting in January 2017, which I will attend, but I feel that I will not be recruited onto the board. Similar to the situation with LI UK, I am probably too challenging! I am okay with this, but I sincerely hope

THE MOLES IN OCTOBER

that whoever represents the adoption process is up to the challenge, willing to question and, most importantly, keen to innovate. I am not very hopeful. In my experience, people like to recruit like-minded people who do not challenge or rock the boat and are willing to maintain the status quo.

I think in the case of adoption support, the status quo needs to be jettisoned from the water, shaken up and started afresh. The people leading the RAA process are those who have a vested interest in keeping their jobs and defending their past record. I keep hearing that Stockport has a good track record and that is why they are helping develop the first tranche of RAA development. This could, cynically, be read in a different light! If they were successful, why would they have to reorganise?

One of the people introducing the update stated that an indication of their success in the field of adoption support was that very few adoptions failed, but I believe that this success is due to the resilience and commitment of the adopters. *Adopters who do not give up on their children.* My belief is that this resilience should not be tested to destruction, but that support should be easily and readily accessed. A more flexible, mentoring-type approach, providing tailor-made support could help navigate the ups and downs that adoption presents far more effectively. The introduction of the RAAs was supposed to open up innovation, but, to date, innovation is lacking. I hope that those involved broaden out their perspectives and seek new approaches, even if they challenge the establishment.

Diary: 20/12/16

Today, we attended the Education & Health Care Plan (EHC) review for Eric. Sue Hawkins kindly attended to make sure that Eric's wishes, expressed last week, were heard. I was delighted that his views were heard and will be actioned. The meeting is a fitting end to this book, even though our journey will continue. Eric has surpassed all expectations and he is now attending most of his lessons in the main school, without receiving additional support.

Eric is increasingly able to manage his anger and not retaliate, even when provoked. He can talk about things, move on and not hold grudges against staff or students as he has in the past. Eric is a role model to some of the younger students, he is on the School Council representing the Hub and his red jumper denotes his new position. He is doing the Sport Leadership programme and had to take a class of Year 7 students who were renowned as being "complex" to manage. He did really well, but recognised that it had been hard in that when he asked them to do one thing, they did another!

Eric is managing to identify his triggers and suggest ways around them that may help – for example, he finds the double lesson for the Duke of Edinburgh Award too long and suggested that he would cope better if he could get some fresh air in between or just move around. This will be facilitated for him from now on. He has a girlfriend at school and has maintained a friendship with a young man who used to go to that school for over 18 months. He no longer has to have his hood up at all times. He even went paintballing and loved it!

Eric received a reward for the last day of term to go shopping with £10 from the school fund. He has received a Headmasters' "letter home", commending his attitude to learning and behaviour. Eric is achieving far more academically than we thought possible.

We left the meeting feeling very proud. As I walked to the car with Sue, I realised that our time of working together would be ending very soon, but that I was unable to portray how much her support has meant to us as a family.

Diary: 21/12/16

Derm and I went to Delamere Forest today to walk Pearl. I had a phone call from Andy Ruddick (from the Hub) about Eric. He asked how we felt after the review meeting and I said how pleased we were and how different it felt to this time last year. I thanked him and his staff for all their support. Andy went on to say that he'd had a meeting with CAMHS recently and that they recognised how successful the Hub model was. The Hub has a nurturing approach and, as I have been saying for years, what child would not benefit from that?

I really want those who have helped Eric and our family to know how much they have done. I hope that they read at least some of my book to see that my words are not empty of meaning, but are heartfelt. Our home is calmer, I am calmer, the girls are happier. Derm is able to enjoy retirement and we will celebrate our 25th wedding anniversary (and 30 years together) next June. This is a feat in itself, I feel, but, for us, it is particularly poignant. We have travelled a very difficult path and it is a fact that most couples going through adoption with a complex child – let alone with three children – rarely stay together. We are very much together as we still laugh and still like the same things. We are stronger than ever and that is worth celebrating.

Eric has taught me a lot over the last 12 years. I understand complex individuals and realise that, without my curiosity and drive to "do better", I would have admitted defeat years ago. Mum always said that he was my cross to bear, but also that she could envision him as an adult, towering over me, with his arm over my shoulders. This is not too far from the truth now!

We are still a work-in-progress, but aren't we all? For the first time, I do feel hope for our future. I feel that Eric can forge his place in this world, knowing that we are always there for him.

21

ERIC IN THE ROUND

I believe that I have acquired some answers along the way and some of the labels I hate so much have proven to be useful in some respects – I still do not have to like them! The main thing that I have learnt is that Eric is a complex individual and does not fit into a box. This is why he is so challenging, but it is also what makes him unique and intriguing. This complexity is what has made parenting him so very difficult, as no one strategy was ever sufficient. Each intervention might work for a brief time, but then its effectiveness would disappear. Set formulaic interventions were always doomed to failure.

Eric has autism and this explains some of his thinking, but his complexity is such that he is not always autistic and he does not always present as such. This takes you off-guard. He seems to float in and out of this condition and that is why I struggle so much with this label because autism is fixed for most people, but not for my son! I can have an ordinary conversation with him and then, out of nowhere, the traits of autism catch me off guard. The intransigent thinking, the concrete immovable views of the world, hit me head on. The art of reason is lost until the thinking Eric re-emerges.

Eric has 90% ADHD and this is controlled with medication that is classified as being a Class A drug. I would still like to see if research in neuropsychology can address this condition in a less dramatic manner because the long-term effects of these medications is not fully understood. The ADHD label helps people understand why Eric cannot concentrate for long periods of time. It helps others understand him a bit better and perhaps be a bit more forgiving.

Eric has Pathological Demand Avoidance (undiagnosed) and hates to be told or asked what to do. I am trying to let him see that bringing his washing down is not a sign of failure, but that we can create a "win/win" situation. This understanding of his character helps manage him with less conflict, but, obviously, it does not fully eradicate it.

Eric needs to be liked and the Hub at school was just what he needed. Without the autistic label, he could not have gone into that teaching environment. Without the autistic label, he would not have been entitled to one-to-one support for four hours a week – the only activity independent from us that he can take part in.

Eric needed a special school with small classes, not a learning disability school. He needed to be understood in order to excel. Unfortunately, mainstream schools could not accommodate him and this is still difficult for him and myself. For me, it is a loss; for him, he is always in a volatile environment that exacerbates his anxiety because he is often hit by other students. The environment he is now is the best that we could hope for and we hope that he can achieve all that he is able to in the future.

22

IN CONCLUSION

Life with Eric has been a roller-coaster ride. I believe that the journey could have been less traumatic if some of the people we met along the way were more professional, more empathic. We all needed support and help, but accessing this support meant that I was in conflict with the powers that be from the outset.

Adoption is a difficult choice to make and trauma and attachment issues are bound to surface at some time or other. Unfortunately, in Eric's case, we faced attachment issues and other inhibitors that shook our whole family to its very core. It could be argued that no parent knows how their child will turn out, but add SEN and adoption into the mix and the path is going to be challenging in the extreme. I feel that we were let down by the system. We needed more specialised support, but it was not forthcoming. It was hard enough parenting

IN CONCLUSION

Eric, without having to fight all of the external battles as well. It felt like a war was raging on all fronts. Adoption should not be this hard.

My experience has taught me that a more versatile, responsive service is needed for post-adoption support. Empathy is required as a given with all practitioners. Support should be provided when it is actually needed in the shape of an experienced individual who is warm and knowledgeable. They do not have to be social workers, in fact, I would have benefitted from a "buddy" or a mentor to help me weave my way through the maze that is the Post-Adoption Support Fund. It is time for the support on offer to become more creative than ever before, especially in light of all the funding cuts. Better does not always mean more expensive.

I believe that all adopters and adopted children should be able to access this support and therapy. Attachment issues can now be healed with new therapeutic interventions, such as Lifespan Integration Therapy. Trauma and secondary trauma can be treated and resolved. The knowledge is out there: but the gatekeepers to the funding streams need to become more aware of the possibilities that now exist.

At the present time, organisations such as the Post Adoption Centre (PAC-UK) have become more recognised in the wake of the RAA being developed. They provide a great resource for adopters. However, this and other organisations also insist that they conduct extensive assessments of the family unit before recommending interventions. This process is extremely expensive and, therefore, prohibitive to many. One family I know have been sent from one screening test to another for over two years and still no therapy has been recommended or given.

The model that we had in the end was far better. The assessment was done and this took too long, but once an experienced professional got involved with our family, support was given in a constructive manner. Therapeutic intervention occurred and this fundamentally altered our son, our daughter, our life.

Everyone faced with attachment issues or post-adoption difficulties should be able to access this help before a crisis occurs. As with all things, prevention is better than cure. If we had accessed this support earlier, then the toll on us all would have been far less: Eric could have thrived before now; I would not have been traumatised; the allegation would not have been made; my family would not have nearly crumbled.

This model could be rolled out, using mentors, buddies in the guise of experienced adopters, not just people who have read about it. Experienced counsellors could provide the support and the therapeutic interventions cost-effectively with the right training. Improvements to service provision do not necessarily have to equate to more money being spent, just that the money available is wisely spent.

A lot of individuals along the way have made the road travelled rockier than it needs to be, but a few brilliant individuals have restored my faith!

ABOUT THE AUTHOR

Laura Morrissey worked as a police constable and sergeant for seven years and then worked as a manager in two charities, Alternative Futures and Mencap, supporting individuals with learning disabilities in the community and developing new services. She took a break from her career to adopt three children. Eric, the youngest, was adopted by Laura and her husband, Dermot, in 2004. The subsequent issues raised by parenting an 'attachment disordered' child meant that her career break became permanent and the search for answers led to a whole new career in the world of counselling. Laura is now qualified as an Accredited Integrative Counsellor, specialising in Attachment and Trauma and she uses Lifespan Integration Therapy in her practice.

Through a desire to be the best parent that she could be and because of her forever-curious mind, Laura researched new approaches and developments that would help her son. Eric acquired many labels on his journey through education, but essentially Laura wanted others facing similar difficulties to know that they are not alone and that there are some answers out there. The result is this book and through it she hopes her experiences can help others to find more direct routes to those solutions.

Loving Eric is a book about Adoption, Attachment, Autism and ADHD. It describes the challenges faced by Laura's family and provides some answers and new therapeutic approaches that really work. It provides hope for others and possibly enlightenment for professionals working in any of these fields.

GLOSSARY

Attachment

'Attachment theory... (a set of concepts that explain the emergence of an emotional bond between an infant and primary caregiver and the way in which this bond affects the child's behavioral and emotional development into adulthood.'

www.dictionary.com/browse/attachment-theory

ADHD

'Attention Deficit Hyperactivity Disorder (ADHD) is a group of behavioural symptoms that include inattentiveness, hyperactivity and impulsiveness.'

http://www.nhs.uk/conditions/Attention-deficit-hyperactivity-disorder/Pages/Introduction.aspx

Autism

'Autism is a lifelong developmental disability that affects how people perceive the world and interact with others.'

http://www.autism.org.uk/autism

Child and Adolescent Mental health Services (CAMHS)

'They offer assessment and treatment when children and young people have emotional, behavioural or mental health difficulties.'

http://www.youngminds.org.uk/for_parents/services_children_young_people/camhs/what_are_cahms

Educational Psychologists (E.P.)

'Educational psychologists help children or young people who are experiencing problems that hinder their successful learning and participation in school and other activities. These problems can include a range of emotional and social problems or learning difficulties.'

https://www.prospects.ac.uk/job-profiles/educational-psychologist

Eye Movement Desensitisation and Reprocessing (EMDR)

'(Is an).integrative psychotherapy approach that has been extensively researched and proven effective for the treatment of trauma.'

http://www.emdria.org/?page=2

Special Educational Needs (SEN)

'Special Educational Needs (SEN) is a legal term. It describes the needs of a child who has a difficulty or disability which makes learning harder for them than for other children their age.'

http://www.bbc.co.uk/schools/parents/identifying_sen/

Speech and Language Therapy (S & LT)

'Speech and Language Therapy is concerned with the management of disorders of speech, language, communication and swallowing in children and adults.'

http://www.westerntrust.hscni.net/services/2506.htm

REFERENCES

Barish, K. (2012). *Pride and Joy: Understanding your child's emotions and solving family problems. http://www. psychologytoday.com/blog/pride-and-joy/201205/ understanding-children-s-emotions-pride-and-shame*

Biehal, N., Ellison, S., Wade, J., Sinclair, I., Dixon, J., Richards, A. (2011). Social Policy Research Unit, University of York, 'Belonging and Permanence: Outcomes in long-term foster care and adoption'. *http://adoptionresearchinitiative.org.uk/summaries/ ARi_summary_1.pdf*

Bowlby, J. (1969). *Attachment and Loss, Attachment: Vol. 1 / Attachment and Loss, Loss: Vol. 3.* New York: Basic Books. *http://www.abebe.org.br/wp-content/uploads/ John-Bowlby-Attachment-Second-Edition-Attachment-and-Loss-Series-Vol-1-1983.pdf*

Callahan, T., & Keefer Smalley, B. (2009). *Wounded Children, Healing Homes: How Traumatized Children Impact Adoptive and Foster Families. books.google.co.uk/ books?isbn=1615215220*

Gobbel, R.. *Trauma is Contagious.* Gobbel Counselling & Adoption Services. *http://gobbelcounseling.wordpress. com/2014/04/21/trauma-is-contagious/*

Gray, D. (2012). *Nurturing Adoptions: Creating Resilience after Neglect and Trauma. books.google.co.uk/books?isbn=085700607X*

Lopez Levers, L. (2012). *Trauma Counselling: Theories and Interventions. books.google.co.uk/books?isbn=0826106838*

Pecora et al., (2005). *Findings from the Northwest Foster Care Alumni Study. www.casey.org/resources/publications/.../improvingfamilyfostercare_fr.p*

Quick, D.E., (2009). *The Healing Journey for Adult Children of Alcoholics. http://books.google.co.uk5ucmOC&pg=PA56&dq=children+who+feel+shame&hl=en&sa=X&ei=Z3CU9qsIsWbO_S7geAO&ved=0CCUQ6AEwAQ#v=onepage&q=children%20who%20feel%20shame&f=false*

Rushton, A., Monck. E.. *Enhancing Adoptive Parenting: A randomised controlled trial of adoption support.* Thomas Coram Research Unit, Institute of Education, University of London. *http://adoptionresearchinitiative.org.uk/summaries/ARi_summary_11.pdf*

Saakvitne, Pearlman and Staff of TSI/CAAP (Norton, 1996). *Transforming the Pain: A Workbook on Vicarious Trauma. books.google.co.uk/books?isbn=0826106838*

Van der Kolk, B. (2005). *Developmental Trauma Disorder: Toward a rational diagnosis for children with complex trauma histories. http://www.traumacenter.org/products/Developmental_Trauma_Disorder.pdf*

USEFUL REFERENCES & READING

1. Ainsworth, M. D. S., Blehar, M. C., Waters, E., & Wall, S. (1978). *Patterns of Attachment: A psychological study of the strange situation*, Hillsdale, NJ: Erlbaum.

2. Attachment & Reactive Attachment Disorders (http://www.helpguide.org)

3. Bowlby, J. (1951). *Maternal Care and Mental Health*. World Health Organization Monograph.

4. Bowlby, J. (1953). *Child Care and the Growth of Love*. London: Penguin Books

5. Cherry, K. (2016). The Importance of Early Emotional Bonds *https://www.verywell.com/what-is-attachment-theory-2795337*

6. McLeod, S., & John Bowlby (2007). *Maternal Deprivation Theory*, Simply Psychology.

7. Schaffer, H. R., & Emerson, P. E. (1964). *The development of social attachments in infancy*. Monographs of the Society for Research in Child Development. 29, 94.

Made in the USA
Columbia, SC
10 September 2017